Spying on America

SPYING ON AMERICA

The FBI's Domestic Counterintelligence Program

JAMES KIRKPATRICK DAVIS

PRAEGER

New York
Westport, Connecticut
London

Copyright Acknowledgment

The author and publisher gratefully acknowledge permission to reprint extracts from the following:

Clarence M. Kelley and James Kirkpatrick Davis, *Kelley: The Story of an FBI Director* (Kansas City, Mo.: Andrews, McMeel, and Parker, 1987). By permission of Universal Press Syndicate.

Library of Congress Cataloging-in-Publication Data

Davis, James Kirkpatrick.
    Spying on America : the FBI's domestic counterintelligence program / James Kirkpatrick Davis.
      p.   cm.
    Includes bibliographical references and index.
    ISBN 0-275-93407-1 (alk. paper)
    1. United States. Federal Bureau of Investigation. 2. Political crimes and offenses—United States—Investigation—History—20th century. 3. Political persecution—United States—History—20th century.   I. Title.
HV8144.F43D38   1992
364.1'32'0973—dc20   91-23131

British Library Cataloguing in Publication Data is available.

Library of Congress Catalog Card Number: 91-23131
ISBN: 0-275-93407-1

First published in 1992

Praeger Publishers, One Madison Avenue, New York, NY 10010
An imprint of Greenwood Publishing Group, Inc.

Printed in the United States of America

The paper used in this book complies with the Permanent Paper Standard issued by the National Information Standards Organization (Z39.48-1984).

10 9 8 7 6 5 4 3 2 1

For Nancy, Whitney, and Carter Davis

Contents

Acknowledgments

I am indebted to a number of individuals who kindly provided me with valuable assistance in preparing this book.

Clarence M. Kelley, former FBI Director and Kansas City Chief of Police, offered much needed encouragement and advice. Edward S. Miller, Deputy Associate FBI Director (Retired), and Special Agent James P. Hosty, Jr. (Retired) provided expert commentary based on their years of experience with the bureau.

William C. Davidon, Professor of Mathematics at Haverford College; Professor Thomas E. Ingerson, Tucson, Arizona; Reverend Edwin Edwards, United Church of Christ in New Haven, Connecticut; Dennis G. Kuby, Ministry of Ecology in Berkeley, California; and Eugene Kaza of Portland, Oregon, were all helpful in providing their firsthand impressions of the many COINTELPRO operations.

The Franklin D. Roosevelt Library in Hyde Park, New York, supplied information on the beginnings of FBI domestic counterintelligence operations.

Information on the actual beginnings of COINTELPRO and deliberations within the Eisenhower administration came from the Dwight D. Eisenhower Library in Abilene, Kansas.

Ted Gittinger, a researcher at the Lyndon Baines Johnson Foundation in Austin, Texas, gathered data for me, as did Gary M. Stern, research associate at the Center for National Security Studies.

Jan Shinpoch, Director of Administrative Operation at the National Security Archive in Washington, D.C., researched archive files and made hundreds of FBI counterintelligence documents available to me in manageable form.

I am also indebted to John M. Pfeffer, Librarian with the Data Base and Newspaper Center of the Free Library of Philadelphia.

Carl Stern, Law Correspondent with NBC News, was the first journalist to pursue the COINTELPRO story. Mr. Stern provided me with a great deal of information and documents, including his firsthand knowledge of COINTELPRO.

Joan Murray and the staff of Inform at the Minneapolis Public Library kindly fulfilled many requests for newspaper and periodical data. I also received help from Steve Binns of the Linda Hall Library in Kansas City, Missouri, and from the government documents librarians at the General Library located on the University of Missouri at Kansas City campus.

Background information for much of the text was provided by the many capable librarians at the Inter Library Loan Department, Kansas City Public Library.

John T. Elliff, a political scholar based in Washington, D.C., read the final chapter and gave me the benefits of his many years of study. Professor Tony G. Proveda at the State University of New York in Plattsburg, an expert in the study of the FBI, was very helpful.

Susan Cowlback, an editorial assistant at the *New Times* in Phoenix, researched their files for background data on a selected COINTELPRO target. Typing and manuscript editing was very capably handled by Mylene Larson Brinson, Marti L. Hill, Margaret Nevin, Diane Gross, and Kelly Scanlon. Captain Tom Moore, U.S. Marine Corps (Retired), made several excellent suggestions for the book. Many thanks to Mary Glenn, my editor at Praeger Publishers.

Spying on America

1 The Media Office Raid: Secret FBI Counterintelligence Becomes Public

They are experts at saying you have to talk to "A" about
that and "A" says you have to talk to "B" about it and it
becomes obvious soon that nobody is going to talk to you.

Robert D. Cross
President, Swarthmore College

On the night of March 8, 1971, a small group of burglars—almost certainly antiwar activists—carefully made their way to the corner of Front Street and South Avenue in the Philadelphia suburb of Media, Pennsylvania. They probably paused to glance at the Delaware County Courthouse and then focused their attention on an innocuous-looking privately owned office/apartment complex across the street.

This complex housed the local resident office of the Federal Bureau of Investigation, under the direction of Senior Resident Agent Thomas F. Lewis. Neither the building nor the FBI office had an alarm system. The group knew this. They had planned their mission with the greatest of care. Hastening to the front door, they broke into the building with very little effort and headed up the stairs in what must have been almost total silence. The door to the FBI office presented no problems and they moved inside. Knowing exactly what to look for, the burglars avoided the large safe located in the middle of the offices and, with the use of crowbars and perhaps tire irons, they opened and emptied desks and filing cabinets containing an enormous selection of highly classified domestic intelligence documents. They were probably in the FBI office for less than an hour. Then, under cover of darkness, they fled.

The burglars, who called themselves the Citizens' Commission to Investigate the FBI, had taken about 1,000 classified documents with them. These papers dealt primarily with secret FBI intelligence operations that were being conducted throughout the United States—operations begun in 1956, the details of which had been known (until the night of the burglary) only to selected individuals within the FBI. Neither the public nor the news media knew anything about them. Within the FBI, these programs were known by the acronym "COINTELPRO"—that is, counterintelligence programs.

The burglary of an FBI office was a serious matter. A case of break-and-entry and theft. A flagrant violation of federal law.

Nevertheless, the Citizens' Commission obviously felt that the FBI's clandestine intelligence operations were reprehensible. They must have felt that such operations served no useful purpose in a democratic society and, indeed, that such programs were inconsistent with the very fundamentals of a democracy. Thus, they no doubt felt, it was necessary for them to break the law in order to expose a program that was, in fact, a violation of the law.

And so they did.

On March 9, 1971, Mark Felt, a twenty-nine-year veteran with the FBI, was in New York on a routine field office inspection. As chief inspector of the FBI, he was widely known, and he had earned the trust of J. Edgar Hoover. One of Felt's primary responsibilities was the physical security of fifty-nine FBI field offices and 538 resident agencies nationwide. It was a big job. FBI security had been made far more difficult by the volatile temper of the times and, as Felt well knew, there was the constant threat of strong social and political protest—sometimes extremely violent—generated, for the most part, by the war in Vietnam. As a result, the FBI was constantly on edge.

On this particular morning, Felt had just gotten out of his hotel room bed when he received an urgent call from the New York field office night supervisor. He quickly picked up the receiver. "Mr. Felt, the bureau wants you to call as soon as possible," the supervisor said, "and they want you to call on the secure line."

"This sounds ominous," Felt thought.

An FBI sedan picked him up in a matter of minutes and hurried to the New York field office, where Felt quickly put through the secure-line call to Edward S. Miller, his top assistant at the Inspection Division in Washington. Ed Miller was on the line almost immediately. He sounded anxious.

"Mark," he said, "what we feared has finally happened. A group of burglars broke into the Resident Agency at Media, Pennsylvania, near Philly, last night. Apparently they got away with a lot of serials." (Within the Bureau, FBI file documents are called "serials.")

Miller sounded concerned. He quickly outlined for his boss what he knew of the episode, and he gave his assessment. The conversation went back and forth for several minutes. Felt respected Miller's opinion on security matters, and he listened carefully. Then, Ed Miller advised Felt that the director wanted to talk to him as soon as possible. With that, the conversation ended.

"There is no doubt," thought Felt, "our worst fears are now realized." He had halfway expected that something like this might happen, particularly since a number of draft boards had already been raided and there had actually been an unsuccessful robbery attempt at another FBI office. But now that it had actually happened to the FBI, Felt was truly stunned. "Hoover will be livid," he said to himself.

He then called J. Edgar Hoover at FBI headquarters in Washington. The FBI director sounded alarmed but very much in control. By 1971, Hoover had been FBI director for forty-seven years, and he no doubt thought that he had seen just about everything. But the Media episode was something new. Hoover's FBI had been violated. And as a result, his language was extraordinarily colorful. He said that this episode represented an incredible and outrageous breach of FBI security and he would not stand for it. He informed Felt that laboratory and fingerprint people were already at the Media resident office, and he told Felt to go to Media immediately, review the situation, assess its possible ramifications, and have a memo on his desk the next day.

Mark Felt was on a plane to Philadelphia within the hour.

He was met at the Media office by Tom Lewis. The atmosphere was tense. The violation of an FBI office was an aberration, indeed. Lewis was nervous. Everyone sensed the gravity of what had happened. FBI technicians were everywhere. Felt surveyed the situation very carefully, discussed his findings with the headquarter's technical people, and took careful notes. He talked with Tom Lewis for several minutes and then said, "Okay, Tom, let's see what you have in the safe."

Lewis worked the combination dial and then slowly opened the big steel doors. Felt peered inside and was so thunderstruck that he was practically speechless. The safe contained only routine materials such as handbooks, handcuffs, some two-way radios, and nothing more. There had not been a single classified document in the safe! The stolen documents had been largely unprotected in desks and filing cabinets.

Mark Felt later recalled that "Hoover was enraged over the Media burglary and so was I." Felt also said at the time, prophetically, that "the raid" was a dramatic turning point in the image of the FBI.[1]

Hoover's reaction was swift.

Within three days, Tom Lewis was transferred to the Atlanta field office. He also received a scorching letter of censure from Hoover. In addition, Lewis's salary was suspended for thirty days—a particularly painful punishment for a father of six.

Within 120 days of the burglary, Hoover ordered the closing of more than 100 of the FBI's 538 resident agencies.[2] Also, sophisticated alarm systems were installed in all remaining bureau resident agencies not located in well-guarded and secure buildings. No action of this type was taken concerning the bureau's fifty-nine field offices; but filing procedures for classified domestic intelligence documents, and security operations as well, were changed dramatically in all offices nationwide.

An interesting aspect of this affair concerns the fact that the Media office security arrangements had somehow been approved by an FBI inspection team the year before. Also, Philadelphia Special Agent-in-charge Joe D. Jamison had approved Media security arrangements within the past year.[3]

Within the borough of Media, public reaction was generally sympathetic to the FBI. As James T. Loughran, the borough secretary, said, "Most people see the burglary as harassment of the FBI. It's a shame!" Veteran Carl E. Mau felt that "people are shocked that anyone would have the nerve to fool around with the FBI." Sheriff Paul J. McKinney, whose office was directly across the street in the Delaware County Courthouse, said, "People feel sorry for Tom Lewis." When approached at his home by a reporter, Tom Lewis was obviously not able to express his real feelings. "I'm sorry," he said. "I can't say a thing. I'm sure you understand."

A very different view was expressed by peace activist Robert L. Anthony when he commented, "I am opposed to the FBI spying on people."[4]

In the meantime, Hoover quickly moved ahead with the FBI's massive investigation of the episode. He summoned to Washington one of the most experienced investigators in the bureau: Special Agent Roy K. Moore. Moore was immediately placed in charge of a team of more than 100 special agents, and the resources of one of the world's largest investigative organizations were placed at his disposal. This small army had but one assignment: to find the Citizens' Commission. Whatever the cost.

The operation was among the largest investigations the FBI had ever conducted up to that time. In terms of size and scope, the Patty Hearst kidnapping, Wounded Knee, and Watergate would ultimately be considerably larger—and all three were ultimately successful. But because it represented the first pure concentration of the FBI's very considerable resources, the Media investigation is equally significant in FBI history. It was, however, doomed from the start.

Special agents were instructed to investigate every conceivable Media office lead, with close attention to be directed toward individuals who had been involved in any way with draft board break-ins. Members of the Catholic left, campus radicals, antiwar protestors of every description, and selected members of the academic community were also targets. The gigantic FBI database in Washington was searched for anyone who demonstrated even the most remote possibility of having been involved in an episode such as the Media office raid.

This investigation received the bureau's top priority. Teletype reports were to be submitted to headquarters on a daily basis, and any and all investigative tools were to be used—fingerprint and handwriting analysis, physical surveillance, telephone toll monitoring, confidential informants, and typewriter style analysis. Suspects would not be necessarily eliminated from consideration even if they had not been in Media, Pennsylvania, at the time. Individual interviews with suspects were mandatory.

Nobody had seen the director so worked up before. Hoover personally reviewed the investigation from his working office in Washington, and other investigations were put on hold until the Media case could be solved. The project, which involved thousands of man-hours, went on with great intensity for a year. Special Agent Moore demanded almost superhuman efforts from his team of investigators, who processed thousands of names and interviewed hundreds of individuals.

By utilizing the technical assistance of the Xerox Corporation, FBI investigators were able to determine that intelligence documents released by the Citizens' Commission were being photocopied on the Xerox model 660. However, when this fact was reported in the press, the Citizens' Commission simply changed to another photocopier.

To the FBI's enormous distress, in spite of the gigantic human and technical resources brought to bear, the Citizens' Commission was never found. It was the feeling at the highest levels of the bureau that agents had come close to actual apprehension, and that they may have actually interviewed some members of the Citizens' Commission itself. Ultimately, however, the FBI felt they simply could not muster the necessary evidence to be used in court by government prosecutors.

This investigation, which carried the code name "Medburg," experienced the same extreme difficulty that the FBI was later to encounter in the Patty Hearst and Wounded Knee investigations. In all three cases the FBI was, for the most part, unable to employ its most traditional and effective investigative tool: the use of confidential informants.

The problem with the Medburg investigation was that, while it had been wide ranging in scope, the primary investigative focus had been in eastern Pennsylvania—an area noted for its concentration of educational institutions. Within this area, Powelton Village—a twenty-four-square-block area near the University of Pennsylvania campus—was the main target. Areas such as the Pennsylvania campus were strong focal points of very pronounced anti–Vietnam War sentiment. In 1971 many people in these areas perceived the government as the very institution responsible for a war they felt was criminal and unjust, and they perceived the FBI, in turn, as an institution that utilized clandestine methods to infiltrate and neutralize organizations whose members were simply choosing to exercise their First and Fourth Amendment rights in protest of that war.

In fact, residents in the Powelton area were so enraged by the intrusive presence of the FBI that they brought suit against Attorney General John N. Mitchell and FBI Director Hoover. The bureau was charged with invasion of privacy, intimidation, and specific infringement on the rights of a number of plaintiffs to free speech and association. The network of those who felt this intense antipathy toward the government could not be penetrated. Thus, without informants, all the special agents in the world could not locate the Citizens' Commission.

The case has never been solved.

The first news of the Media office raid appeared in the March 10, 1971, *New York Times*. It was a small article of less than a dozen lines.[5]

On March 11, however, Haverford College physics professor William C. Davidon, a well-known peace activist; *Boston Globe* reporter Michael Kenny, who covered antiwar protest issues for his paper; and the Philadelphia FBI office all received letters from the Citizens' Commission. Professor Davidon read his letter to a somewhat astonished group of about 100 persons assembled at the Swarthmore Presbyterian Church for a regular meeting of the Swarthmore Ministers Association. The Citizens' Commission letter said, in effect, that the FBI documents had been stolen from the Media office so that the nature and extent of FBI surveillance activities in this country could be studied in depth. The letter said the commission was particularly concerned about the fact that FBI surveillance activities were being carried out on a regular basis against "groups and individuals working for a more just, humane, and peaceful society." It went on to say that the FBI files would be studied to determine "how much of the FBI's efforts are spent on relatively minor crimes by the poor and powerless against whom they can get a more glamorous conviction rate, instead of investigating truly serious crimes by those with money and influence which cause great damage to the lives of many people."

Professor Davidon said he had never before heard of the Citizens' Commission to Investigate the FBI. Davidon thought that the letter might have been sent to him because of his strong public stand in support of nonviolence. He was a well-known member of the Peace Division of the American Friends Service Committee. Additionally, Davidon had been named as a coconspirator (but not a defendant)—along with Rev. Daniel C. Berrigan and others—in the alleged and widely publicized "Harrisburg Six" plot to kidnap the president's national security advisor, Henry A. Kissinger.

Davidon claimed he had no regrets about not immediately telling the FBI of the letter, and he most certainly did approve of the raid. When asked later why he approved of the action, the professor said that "the FBI is increasingly engaged in activities which are contrary to the best principles of this country." Davidon said he had chosen to read the letter at this particular meeting because, insofar as he knew, there had been no mention of the FBI raid in the newspapers up to that time.[6]

Davidon remembers the spring of 1971 as a very busy time, since he played a key role in helping to make the Media documents public. "My home telephone was tapped," he recalls, "and I later discovered my name on a number of FBI domestic intelligence documents. The whole value of the Media exposure was to provide some documentation of the extent to which the FBI was infiltrating perfectly legal groups. The FBI under Hoover was becoming dangerously insensitive to people's rights."[7]

The Citizens' Commission letter also said that, after its study of the files was completed, "documentation" would be sent to "the people in public life who have demonstrated the integrity, courage, and commitment to democratic values which are necessary to effectively challenge the repressive policies of the FBI." The commission concluded by saying that it felt the citizens of this country had the right to control their own government and that the FBI had quite simply betrayed the public trust.

Thus, the first public exposure of COINTELPRO—however faint— began with the outright public allegation that the FBI had spent insufficient time and effort in combating the "war profiteering, monopolistic practices, institutionalized racism, organized crime and the mass distribution of lethal drugs."[8]

After the public reading of the Citizens' Commission letter, all was quiet in the news media for about ten days. Then, carefully selected copies of about twenty of the stolen documents were sent to Congressman Parren J. Mitchell of Maryland and Senator George S. McGovern of South Dakota. Both men were Democrats, and both had been publicly critical of the FBI.

McGovern returned the material to the bureau immediately, saying that he "refused to be associated with this illegal action by a private group. Illegal actions of this nature only serve to undermine reasonable and constructive efforts to secure appropriate public review of the FBI."[9] Congressman Mitchell was also opposed to the Media burglary; he, too, returned the materials to the FBI. He did say, however, that his review of the file had convinced him that the FBI was involved in some highly unlawful activities, including illegal surveillance and the infiltration of private citizen groups.

Immediately thereafter, in a speech on March 23, Mitchell said that "burglary was a crime and should be dealt with as such. However," he added, "the investigation and surveillance of individuals and peace groups and black student groups as indicated by the files, was also a crime."[10]

Also on March 23, packets containing carefully chosen copies of fourteen of the stolen documents were sent to selected prominent journalists and newspapers, including *New York Times* columnist Tom Wicker, Betty Medsger of the *Washington Post*, and the *Los Angeles Times*. Enclosed with each packet of COINTELPRO documents was a letter from the Citizens'

Commission saying, "We have taken this action because we believe that democracy can survive only in an order of justice, of an open society and public trust, because we believe that citizens have the right to scrutinize and control their own government and because we believe that the FBI has betrayed its democratic trust."[11]

The rapidly developing revelation of the COINTELPRO documents to the public sent shock waves through the halls of the Justice Department, which was deluged with news media requests for more information about the Media burglary and the stolen FBI documents. Attorney General John N. Mitchell was deeply disturbed, Hoover was livid, and it seems certain that the attorney general discussed the matter with President Nixon as well. In a public announcement on March 24, Mitchell said that the stolen documents were highly confidential and should not be published. Mitchell went on to say that publication of these stolen FBI papers "could endanger the lives or cause other serious harm to persons engaged in investigative activities on behalf of the United States. Disclosure of national defense information that might be contained in the papers could endanger the United States and give aid to foreign governments whose interests might be inimical to those of the United States."[12]

At first, the *New York Times* and the *Los Angeles Times* honored the attorney general's request. A spokesman for the Justice Department said there had been intensive conversations between department officials and the editorial staff of the *Washington Post* on March 23. Ben Bagdikian, the *Post's* national editor at the time, received a call directly from John Mitchell. Nevertheless, Bagdikian recalls, "the *Post* thought it was a significant matter of public controversy and once we confirmed that the documents were authentic, we decided to go ahead. It was an insight into something the public needs to know."[13]

Concurrent with the publication of information from the documents, moreover, the *Washington Post* editorialized that "this revelation of FBI activity in the name of internal security seems to us extremely disquieting," and recommended that "an appropriate committee of the Congress ought to look much more thoroughly into what the bureau is doing."[14] When the *Post* published parts of the documents (withholding individual names and locations), the New York and Los Angeles papers immediately followed suit.

In the government's view, these documents had not only been obtained illegally, but had also been published in a manner that was skillfully out of context. Although the approximately 1,000 FBI

COINTELPRO documents covered an extremely wide range of secret investigative activities, the commission (showing editorial skills as well as criminal aptitude) had chosen to release only those specific memos that depicted the bureau's more questionable methods of internal surveillance on the numerous activist groups flourishing during the years from 1956 to 1971, especially during the 1960s.

"Actually," one Justice Department official remembers, "a full examination of the stolen documents reveals that the FBI showed restraint rather than overzealousness. They do excellent police work."[15] This official, however, was seriously underestimating just how far the FBI had gone: In many cases, basic constitutional guarantees had quite simply been violated.

One of the memos from the first release directed FBI agents to investigate and monitor groups organized to meet the demands of certain black activist students. This particular memo, dated November 4, 1970, claimed that "increased campus disorders involving black students pose a definite threat to the nation's stability and security and indicate need for increases in both the quality and quantity of intelligence information on Black Student Unions [BSUs] and similar groups which are targets for influence and control by the violence-prone Black Panther Party (BPP) and other extremists." Hoover also specified in this memo that "this program will include junior colleges and two year colleges as well as four year colleges."[16]

Another document, dated September 16, 1970, contained a newsletter called "The New Left Notes—Philadelphia." This newsletter had been produced by Special Agent James O'Connor, from the New Left desk at the Philadelphia FBI field office. Its first issue (dated September 9) instructed agents to intensify contacts with radicals and dissidents so as to enhance "the paranoia endemic in these circles and to further serve to get the point across that there is an FBI agent behind every mail box." In addition, the newsletter continued, "some will be overcome by the overwhelming personalities of the contacting agent and volunteer to tell all—perhaps on a continuing basis."[17]

A third memo discussed the recruiting of college student informers between the ages of eighteen and twenty-one to report campus extremists to the FBI.[18] Operating within a network of other informants at their college—including college staff personnel, postal employees, and local police, all feigning to be supporters of the cause—the informants would provide information to the FBI, and the bureau would then do its utmost to embarrass and disrupt the extremists.

All in all, this did not paint an attractive picture of the internal thinking—and procedures—of the FBI at that time. But the armed violence of some on-campus militants and of certain others in the American streets wasn't very pretty either. The Citizens' Commission, of course, chose to ignore the fact that rebellious activities were making the FBI's presence on campuses and in the streets necessary in the first place.

Throughout this period, the FBI's extensive efforts seemed to be intended to keep in balance—"to neutralize"—the seething unrest in colleges, college towns, and cities throughout the land. One of the stolen documents referred to surveillance of Dr. William Bennett, a philosophy instructor at Swarthmore College. The FBI evidently suspected Dr. Bennett of harboring two fugitives—Katherine Powers of Detroit and Susan E. Saxe of Atlanta. Both women had been placed on the FBI's "most wanted" list in October 1970. They were part of a radical revolutionary group located in the Boston area and were suspected of being involved in a Boston-area robbery in which a policeman had been killed in September 1970. Bennett was contacted at his home by two FBI agents to determine if he knew anything about the Boston robbery. He denied any knowledge.

In addition, Bennett had invited a Black Panther party official to speak at Swarthmore College once in 1970, and he had also been quite active in the "Radical Circus"—a radical group of college students and faculty who were active in the civil rights and anti–Vietnam War movements. Evidently, many of his actions had been taken without consulting college administrators and, as a result, he had been the subject of criticism from college officials.

In their surveillance of Bennett, special agents enlisted the help of a local police chief, a switchboard operator, and a college security officer. The switchboard operator was used to monitor and report on long distance calls that Bennett received. When he was later told that he had been under surveillance by the Federal Bureau of Investigation, Bennett responded, "Sometimes you get the feeling that the FBI has everybody under surveillance."[19] Bennett recalled later that "the whole surveillance thing by the FBI is a way of inventing paranoia in people carried out by penny novel spy tactics."[20]

Commenting on this investigation, Swarthmore College President Robert D. Cross said that the institution was in the process of drafting a policy to cover such matters. It would say, in effect, that "the college will not divulge any of its personnel records to government agencies including the FBI or personal records of students and faculty without the student or faculty member first knowing or seeing the information."[21]

Cross then telephoned Hoover for an explanation of the FBI surveillance at the college. "They are experts," Cross reported, "at saying you have to talk to 'A' about that and 'A' says you have to talk to 'B' about it and it becomes obvious soon that nobody is going to talk to you."[22]

Following his effort to talk to Hoover, Cross sent a letter to the FBI, asking them either to authenticate or else to deny the FBI surveillance at Swarthmore. He received no reply. "To be perfectly candid," the college president later said, "I didn't expect any."[23]

Three documents from those released on March 23 mentioned the Philadelphia Black Panthers, the National Black Economic Development Conference (BEDC), and Muhammad Kenyatta, the BEDC's national vice-president. (The National Black Economic Development Conference is the organization that, in 1969, called for the nation's primarily white churches to pay reparations to blacks for past racial injustices.)

When Kenyatta obtained the released Media documents referring to him and his organization, he strongly criticized the FBI for its efforts to infiltrate and subvert civil rights and peace organizations. He said that he knew informants had been planted within his group, and that he had told them to get out of the BEDC altogether.

The three documents included one (dated July 13, 1970) concerning Kenyatta's unlisted telephone number. There was also a six-page memo (dated June 18, 1970) concerning the FBI's use of a bank officer—Daniel McGronigle, a cashier at Southeast National Bank—to monitor the BEDC checking account.

Checking account information is normally confidential, of course. However, McGronigle later explained that the bank had not released information on BEDC financial affairs to the FBI until a special agent presented him with a court order to do so.

The very idea that the FBI could gain access to a citizen's private financial affairs was quite astounding to many Americans. This practice was not new, however, nor was it limited to COINTELPRO operations. Columnist Jack Anderson, in testifying before the Senate Banking Committee in 1972, said "informants inside the FBI" had told him that "the practice of examining checking accounts of people under surveillance was widespread." Anderson's research into the background files of Jane Fonda, Dr. Benjamin Spock, and Floyd B. McKissick demonstrated that, when investigating political activists, the FBI "has virtually unlimited access to private bank account records."[24]

Interestingly enough, at a March 24 press conference in Philadelphia, BEDC's Kenyatta said he had seen the three documents that mentioned him *before* they had been made public. When asked by a reporter how this was possible, Kenyatta replied, "Let it suffice to say that the revolutionary information networks are growing all across America. [B]oth sides can play the *I Spy* game."[25]

Kenyatta went on to express his rage about the FBI's infiltration of his organization. "For too long," he said, "J. Edgar Hoover, Attorney General John Mitchell and Richard M. Nixon and others of their kind have squandered taxpayers' hard earned dollars to pay two-bit informants to tap private telephones, to hire agent provocateurs and to purchase *Mission Impossible* type electric surveillance devices."[26]

When asked if the BEDC had any connection with the Citizens' Commission to Investigate the FBI, Kenyatta said, "We are grateful for their existence. God bless them."[27]

Still another black organization, the Black United Liberation Front (BULF), was also a target of FBI infiltration. In fact, FBI penetration of this organization was so complete that one informant was close enough to say, "The BULF is not going to buy a type setting machine. They are buying an electric typewriter and are supposed to have the use of a type setter; the location of which she [the informant] does not know."[28]

Another FBI memo was related to the convening of the War Resisters Conference at Haverford College on August 1, 1969. The memo directed to its addressees several inquiries concerning the conference aimed at determining "its scope and whether or not there are any indications it will generate any anti-US propaganda."[29]

Also included were instructions on infiltrating the 1970 National Association of Black Students Convention, to be held at Detroit's Wayne State University.[30] In still another memo, there was a Swarthmore Police Department report on black militant activities at Swarthmore College.

The small initial group of documents released by the commission suggested that there had been far more extensive surveillance of the political left by the FBI than had generally been known. Additionally, it was revealed that there had been a continuous FBI surveillance of students, teachers, and scientists who had been to the Soviet Union for more than a month, to determine if there had been attempts by Soviet intelligence to recruit them.

It has long been suspected—though never proven—that one of the principal purposes of the Media raid was to try to acquire the primary federal documents involving the Harrisburg Six. This group, of which Rev. Philip F. Berrigan was a member, was indicted by a federal grand jury in Harrisburg, on January 12, 1971, on charges of conspiring to kidnap Dr. Henry A. Kissinger and to blow up heating systems in government buildings.

In an article by Joe O'Dowd and Jon Katz of the *Philadelphia News*, it was pointed out that the FBI knew, immediately after the Media raid, that duplicate copies of the entire government case against the Harrisburg Six had been stolen. Copies of these documents had almost certainly been put in the hands of associates of Reverend Berrigan. As the article said, the "crux" of the government case had been stolen.[31] Sources said that one of the main functions of the FBI Media office had been to investigate coconspirators in the Harrisburg Six case and thus build a stronger case against Berrigan and his people. Ostensibly, this is why these important files were stored in Media: to enable special agents to refer to persons and data in the documents that were already a part of the government case.

On March 26, the Citizens' Commission demonstrated a change in its publicity strategy. A Philadelphia reporter received a letter from the Citizens' Commission that read thus: "In a few days we will contact a first group of these previously undercover agents and suggest they cease their repressive actions if they have not already done so. We will then inform those individuals and any organizations against whom these agents were operating. Following that we will make the names of the first group of agents public."[32]

A few days later, still another domestic intelligence episode was revealed. Some of the most unusual and bizarre information to come out of the original press set of fourteen documents concerned the matter of Thomas E. Ingerson, a thirty-two-year-old Boy Scout leader from Moscow, Idaho, who planned to take his six-member Boy Scout troop on a camping tour of the Soviet Union in the summer of 1971. On November 4, 1970, Ingerson, an associate professor of physics at the University of Idaho, had written a letter to the Soviet Embassy in which he said that he and his scout troop would like to visit camps of the Soviet scouts—the Pioneers—and also Komsomol Youth Camps.

It came as a considerable surprise to Ingerson when Fred Graham of the *New York Times* called and asked if he knew how his letter found its way into the intelligence files in Media, Pennsylvania. Dr. Ingerson said that he had no idea, but he did know that his letter had been forwarded to Philadelphia's Astro Travel Service, a firm that routinely handled travel requests for the Soviet Union. In 1970, Astro had handled more than 700 such requests.

The *New York Times* called William Nezowy, owner of Astro Travel, and asked him if he or any of his five employees could possibly be supplying travel requests from U.S. citizens for the Soviet Union to the FBI. Nezowy exclaimed, "God, no!"[33]

Shortly after learning of his letter's inclusion in the intelligence files, Ingerson received a call from the Soviet Embassy. The telephone voice, in a heavy Slavic accent, said, "Professor, your visas are denied!" Ingerson was irritated by the call and couldn't imagine what on earth had transpired within the FBI and the Soviet Embassy. "My purpose in writing that letter," he said, "was utterly innocent."[34]

Ingerson was not to be dissuaded, however. He decided to let the dust settle for a few months and then try again. This time—somewhat to his astonishment—he was successful.

"I must have reached a totally different person within the embassy with my second try," Ingerson recalls, "because our visas were processed rather quickly and our group did go on to Russia. In the back of my mind, however, I kept wondering if I was going to hear from the FBI. They never called. To show you what a small world it really is, we ran into some American tourists in Moscow. They said that they had read about our difficulties with the FBI in the newspapers." Ingerson, now with an observatory in Chile, still recalls the incident with some concern and some amusement.

"I never heard from the FBI again. I have never been able to fathom the mind of the FBI. How on earth they could be concerned with a college physics instructor and a group of Boy Scouts is beyond me. I'm sure my name is floating around in an FBI file somewhere."[35]

The Citizens' Commission continued to mail the stolen documents, at a relatively slow pace but to a wider group of recipients. For example, in early April 1971 a new selection (the second mailing) of COINTELPRO documents was sent to an organization in Cambridge, Massachusetts, known as Resist—a group that raised funds for organizations protesting the Vietnam War—and Resist, in turn, made these new documents available to the *New York Times*.

Among these materials, the *Times* discovered an FBI memo in which a lay brother of a Villanova monastery—an FBI informant—reported that a Villanova University priest had borrowed a monastery car for the entire weekend prior to the bombing of the U.S. Capitol. This particular priest turned out to be a known sympathizer of Reverend Berrigan and others who were awaiting trial on federal conspiracy charges.[36]

This second packet of documents also revealed a whole group of COINTELPRO memoranda mailed to all field offices—memos that discussed, at considerable length, the development of a national network of paid FBI informants. Every FBI special agent would be required to develop one "racial informant." Additionally, according to the documents, all information obtained through recruited informants "should be recorded by memo—with copies for the files on any individuals or organizations mentioned."[37]

Ultimately, informants came from many walks of life, including taxi drivers, bartenders, butchers, liquor store proprietors, salespeople, bill collectors, and more. Of particular concern were "the racial informants" utilized to penetrate black militant organizations. Singled out for special observation and informant penetration were the Congress of Racial Equality, the Southern Christian Leadership Conference, and the Black Coalition.

This informant network was designed to intercept extremist activities, such as riots, before they actually took place. Later, however, FBI instructions became much more specific and called for diverting surveillance "into the involvement of black extremists in criminal activities, black militants who attempt to influence the black community, peddlers and purchasers of extremist literature, and efforts by foreign powers to take over the Negro Militant Movement."[38]

It was in this same early-April mailing that the Citizens' Commission made good on its threat to reveal the names of a selected group of FBI informants. Seven individuals were named in the April mailing, which was directed to Senator George S. McGovern, Senator Sam J. Ervin, Jr., and Senator Charles M. Mathers, together with various media contacts.

Along with the documents was a letter in which the Citizens' Commission said, "We regret that this action was necessary, but these are troubled times and the struggle for freedom and justice in this society can never succeed if people continue to betray their brothers and sisters."[39] The informants included a college switchboard operator, various bank employees, and the dean of student affairs at a predominantly black college.

The FBI, of course, had a substantial amount of both time and money invested in working with selected paid informants; and in revealing the identities of these informants, the Citizens' Commission had rendered them useless.

The seizure of buildings at New York's Columbia University in 1968 was discussed in one memo that seems to suggest—reading it today— that FBI thinking had gone completely overboard. According to the memo, the FBI saw the Columbia incident as just the first step in an effort by the extremely radical New Left to seize the industrial power base of the United States. This alarming message had been mailed anonymously to college-level educators and administrators who had failed, in the FBI's opinion, to come to grips with the student activists on their campuses.

Evidence in this mailing also suggests that the FBI was faced with the problem of informants becoming provocateurs. In a memo dated September 16, 1970, the FBI admonished those in the field to be certain that informants "should not become the person who carries the gun, throws the bomb, does the robbery or by some specific violative, overt act becomes a deeply involved participant. There have been cases where security informants assault police, etc."[40]

Some memos from the second and third group of committee mailings today appear fairly bizarre. For example, one memo referred to a man at Rutgers University who was a suspected Black Panther sympathizer. This individual, from Upper Darby, Pennsylvania, had spent part of a semester cutting sugarcane in Cuba as part of the Venceremos Brigade of non-Cubans helping with the harvest. This document, originating from the Newark FBI office, was reprinted in the Rutgers *Targum* and referred to the surveillance target as Dennis Bruskin. Later it was revealed that Dennis Bruskin was actually Denise Bruskin, a Rutgers University coed who had attended one Black Panther meeting and had gone to Cuba more out of curiosity than anything else. In this case the FBI intelligence-gathering machinery, which used a Rutgers campus police officer as informant, had clearly broken down. However, it was certainly clear to everyone, after publication of this document, that the FBI was indeed active in monitoring student activities.

A new set of Media documents—the fourth mailing—was received on or about April 8 by Michael Kenney of the *Boston Globe*.

These documents revealed that the daughter of a member of Congress had been targeted by COINTELPRO. The FBI had conducted surveillance into the activities of Jacqueline Reuss, daughter of Wisconsin Congressman Henry S. Reuss, a longtime outspoken critic of the war in Vietnam. The actual intelligence document was a one-page memorandum dated November 19, 1970, directed to J. Edgar Hoover from the Philadelphia Special Agent-in-charge Joe D. Jamison. The memorandum was entitled "Jacqueline Reuss—Information concerning Security Matters." The security data on Ms. Reuss had been obtained by the FBI from the secretary to the registrar of Swarthmore College—an established FBI source. When contacted by the news media, Ms. Reuss, a twenty-one-year-old senior, said that she "knew that the FBI was checking up on me last fall" and that she assumed the "investigation was the topical sort of thing—leftist activities."[41] She did say that she had belonged to the Students for Democratic Society for about two years, but that she was not at all active and had let her membership expire.

In mid-March, Congressman Reuss was on his way to a meeting of the Asian Development Bank in Singapore. An FBI representative reached him in Tokyo and told him that three documents concerning Jacqueline had been stolen from the Media FBI office and might be made public.

The special agent told Reuss that Swarthmore College, the local police, and a local credit bureau had been checking into some information about Jacqueline originally supplied by another local FBI informant. The congressman was angry about the fact that his daughter had been the target of an FBI intelligence investigation, no matter how ill conceived and poorly considered the operation may have been.

He told reporters in Tokyo on April 12 that "the FBI representative informed me that the investigation had been completed and had developed no information of a derogatory nature concerning Jackie." Reuss then directed several stinging remarks at the bureau. "The FBI," he said, "has an important responsibility to investigate crime. Its mission is not to compile dossiers on millions of Americans, congressmen's daughters or not, who are accused of wrongdoing. They should stick to their mission!"[42]

Still another COINTELPRO document from this fourth mailing contained a report on the internal rivalry between leaders of the Philadelphia Black United Liberation front. The data, which had been provided by a female informant, pointed to suspected bank robbers in the organization, as well as to contacts with the Black Panthers in Philadelphia.

On April 21 the Black Student Union at Pennsylvania Military College (PMC) in Chester, Pennsylvania, received copies of six FBI COINTELPRO documents from the Citizens' Commission—documents explaining that the BSU was under surveillance by the FBI and informants. The black students wanted the information to be made public so that the country would be aware of the FBI's "flagrant use of investigation." BSU member Herb Terrell said that one of the documents listed three FBI informants—a "racial" informant, a PMC security officer, and a Pennsylvania state policeman—by name. After reviewing the documents, PMC President Dr. Clarence R. Moll said, "It is quite evident that the source of information was someone other than our security officer. It would appear that whoever supplied this information to the FBI knew cialist Workers party, the Black Panthers, and almost every other organization that the FBI thought could threaten public tranquility or the security of the government. The domestic files, carefully maintained and enlarged over a period of several years, had come to form a sizable portion of the FBI's data bank in Washington.

The publication of COINTELPRO documents taken from the Media office made Americans keenly aware of the FBI's involvement in the invasion of and loss of individual liberties. Indeed, it was clear that the domestic intelligence activities of the FBI had undergone—to use Theodore White's phrase—an "historic glide"[54] from executive charter for counterintelligence activities to what was essentially a situation in which the COINTELPRO operations, under J. Edgar Hoover's direction, had been accountable to no branch of government at all.

NOTES

1. W. Mark Felt, *The FBI Pyramid* (New York: G. P. Putnam's Sons, 1979), pp. 87–99.

2. Ibid., p. 93.

3. *Evening Bulletin*, Philadelphia, 30 Mar. 1971, p. 64.

4. Donald Janson, "FBI File Theft Stirs Anger and Joy among the Residents of Media, PA," *New York Times*, 29 Mar. 1971.

5. "FBI Reports Office Raid," *New York Times*, 10 Mar. 1971, p. 7.

6. "Davidon Unveils Plot against FBI," *Delaware County Daily Times*, 12 Mar. 1971, pp. 1–2; "Group Claims It Stole FBI Files in Media," *Evening Bulletin*, Philadelphia, 12 Mar. 1971, p. 17.

7. Prof. William C. Davidon, Dept. of Mathematics, Haverford College, telephone interview with author, 26 July 1989.

8. "Davidon Unveils Plot," pp. 1–2.

9. Sanford J. Unger, *FBI: An Uncensored Look behind the Walls* (Boston: Little, Brown, 1975), p. 485.

10. "Mitchell Issues Plea on FBI Files," *New York Times*, 24 Mar. 1971, p. 24.

11. Robert M. Smith, "FBI May Close Smaller Offices," *New York Times*, 14 Apr. 1971, p. 54.

12. "Security Matters," *Facts on File*, 24 Mar. 1971, p. 15.

13. "Radicals, Ripping Off the FBI," *Time*, 5 Apr. 1971, p. 15.

14. Ibid.

15. Betty Medsger and Ken W. Clawson, "Thieves Got Over 1,000 FBI Papers," *Washington Post*, 25 Mar. 1971, p. 1.

16. "Security Matters," *Facts on File*, 24 Mar. 1971, p. 15.

more about the internal workings of the BSU than the security officer does."[43]

The officer in question remembers being approached by special agents in the fall of 1970, but says he declined to provide any information to the FBI. Philadelphia Special Agent-in-charge Joe D. Jamison refused any comment on the matter.

In late March, it was learned that the Philadelphia FBI field office had—according to COINTELPRO documents mailed to the *Philadelphia Bulletin* by the Cambridge organization Resist—recruited eighteen- to twenty-one-year-old New Left informants to work full time or part time. The youths could earn up to $300 per month. "We have been blocked off," the document said, "from this critical age group in the past. Let us take advantage of this opportunity."[44]

In regard to this new revelation, a Resist spokesman said the FBI data once again showed that the information it gathers in a clandestine manner "constitutes a basic violation of the civil rights of both individuals and groups working for social change."[45]

Another disturbing document involved a lifetime conscientious objector who had evidently come to the bureau's attention during a 1967 investigation of antidraft/antiwar activities in the Philadelphia area. The five-page memorandum contained a military school record, police and intelligence unit reports, and interviews with co-workers. According to the documents, this man was described by informants who had worked with him in 1957 at Belleview Medical Center as a "Queer fish or a screwball." A psychiatric report said that he volunteered for certain research experiments, and a psychiatrist's opinion stated that he was altruistic, sincere, believer in God, but not in conventional religion." The profile also revealed he had attended a 1955 meeting of the Proletarian Party of America, distributed antiwar leaflets in Haverford, Pennsylvania, in 1968, and attended antiwar rallies. His attendance at these rallies was described as a "lark."[46] All of these activities are, of course, protected by the First Amendment. He had once broken the law, though, in a minor episode in 1954, which—the record shows—cost him a fine of $5.

It was this sort of bureaucratic nonsense that generated heated criticism of the FBI in the media. Clearly, this individual in no way represented a threat to the security of the government.

Other documents in this fifth packet included evidence of surveillance on the Union for National Draft opposition, as well as files on black students and organizations. This report concluded that the Black Student Union at Pennsylvania Military College was "a somewhat disorganized group of students, possibly having a membership and/or following of no more than 30 students."[47] Again, this surveillance of noncriminals by the FBI created very unfavorable media attention.

By the middle of May 1971, the Citizens' Commission had released a total of sixty domestic intelligence documents, and there were indications that the document release program was coming to an end. No doubt the commission's members were feeling the pressure of the intense FBI investigation to find them.

Reports contained in what was the sixth and final mailing included a profile of the activities of the Jewish Defense League, a report on the surveillance of Klavern 10 of the Ku Klux Klan in Upper Darby, Pennsylvania, and a surveillance report on a peaceful demonstration held in Philadelphia to protest against chemical warfare. It was also learned that the Bell Telephone Company of Pennsylvania had furnished the FBI with "all unlisted telephone subscribers, including the names and addresses, a service not available to ordinary citizens."[48]

In this, its final act, the Citizens' Commission released—together with copies of the final selection of documents—a summary of all the stolen FBI documents. According to the Commission's letter, "30 percent of the materials in the Media files were manuals, routine forms and similar procedural matter."[49] The remainder was comprised of "40% political surveillance and other investigation of political activity. Of these cases two were right wing, ten concerned immigrants, and over 200 were on left or liberal groups. Twenty-five percent bank robberies, twenty percent murder, rape, and interstate theft. Seven percent were draft resisters, including refusal to submit to military induction. Seven percent were leaving the military without government permission. One percent were organized crime, mostly gambling."[50]

News coverage relating to the FBI Media burglary and the incredibly embarrassing exposure of FBI domestic counterintelligence practices was very extensive. For example, in the *New York Times* alone, twenty-four articles on the subject appeared between March 9 and May 23, 1971. Coverage was similarly extensive in virtually all print and broadcast media nationwide, and almost every bit was extremely critical. The FBI had never received such universal condemnation in all its forty-seven-year history.

Fred Graham, a highly respected writer for the *New York Times*, was one of the journalists who followed the story very closely. On May 27 he wrote, "At week's end there was a feeling that the other shoe was yet to drop in the case of the pilfered papers. The question that no one could answer was which side would drop the shoe—the thieves, who obviously have more documents, or the FBI, which has a reputation for producing the facts that give the last word."[51]

However, as the release of documents stopped, media interest also stopped. In fact, by midsummer of 1971, the extraordinarily unfavorable publicity generated by the Media raid had, for all intents and purposes, ceased. In fact, by the end of July, virtually all the major daily papers had stopped running stories about the FBI Media office and the Citizens' Commission to Investigate the FBI.

In any event, the objective of the Citizens' Commission was realize[d] J. Edgar Hoover had become so alarmed over the possibility of havi[ng] to endure even more national exposure that he canceled all COINT[EL]PROs on April 28, 1971.[52]

The actual term "COINTELPRO" was still unknown to the publ[ic at] this point. The only use of the word appeared in one of the ori[ginal] fourteen documents released to the *Washington Post*. This par[ticular] document (containing a newsletter mentioned earlier) wa[s cap]tioned "COINTELPRO–New Left" and was dated September 16, [1970]. In time, this memorandum was to prove extraordinarily import[ant (see] Chapter 7).

In general, the released memoranda revealed a gradual dif[ference] expansion in FBI domestic surveillance activities—an expansio[n that had] been all but completely unknown to the American public. In [the begin]ning—1956—the FBI domestic intelligence operations were [concerned] only with the threat posed by the Communist party. In t[he] documents themselves demonstrated, the FBI surveillance p[rogram ex]panded enormously under J. Edgar Hoover, and soon inc[luded an ex]tremely wide range of racial and political action groups.

For example, in the early years of the civil rights demon[strations the] FBI had looked for foreign (communist) influences within t[he movement.] After the traumatic urban violence of 1960s, however, [as a] result of its extensive penetration of the movement—r[ealized the] civil rights movement was under no foreign influence w[hatsoever—and] yet it still kept up its surveillance of these groups.

Also, as the published documents revealed, the [FBI was] maintaining confidential intelligence files on the Ku [Klux Klan]

17. "Media FBI Records Show Informants," *Delaware County Daily Times*, 24 Mar. 1971, p. 1.

18. Medsger and Clawson, "Thieves."

19. Paul F. Levy and Kitsi Burkhart, "Professor Not Upset by FBI Surveillance," *Philadelphia Bulletin*, 27 Mar. 1971, p. 1.

20. Ibid., p. 2.

21. "Media FBI Records," *Delaware County Daily Times*, p. 2.

22. "Swarthmore College Trustees Condemn Alleged Surveillance," *Delaware County Daily Times*, 5 Apr. 1971, p. 1.

23. Ibid.

24. "Anderson Scores Banks on Records," *New York Times*, 15 Aug. 1972, p. 27.

25. "Kenyatta Shows Copies of Papers Stolen from the FBI," *Evening Bulletin*, Philadelphia, 24 Mar. 1971, p. 1.

26. Ibid.

27. Ibid.

28. FBI Memorandum, Special Agent Richard E. Logan to Philadelphia Special Agent-in-charge, 22 Jan. 1971.

29. Katrina Dyke, "FBI Papers Tell of Watch on Blacks," *Sunday Bulletin*, Philadelphia, 28 Mar. 1971, p. 1.

30. FBI Memorandum, Headquarters to Special Agents, 17 June 1970.

31. Joe O'Dowd and Jon Katz, "Berrigan Plot Evidence Stolen from FBI," *Philadelphia Daily News*, 30 Mar. 1971, p. 3.

32. "Group to Publicize FBI's Informers," *New York Times*, 27 Mar. 1971, p. 32.

33. Fred P. Graham, "Scouts' Letter in FBI Dossiers," *New York Times*, 26 Mar. 1971, p. 27.

34. Prof. Thomas E. Ingerson, Tucson, Ariz., telephone interview with author, June 1989.

35. Ibid.

36. Bill Kovach, "Stolen Files Show FBI Seeks Black Informers," *New York Times*, 8 Apr. 1971, p. 22.

37. Ibid., p. 2.

38. Ibid.

39. Bill Kovach, "A Citizens Commission Writes to Seven Persons Who, It Says, Served as Informants," *New York Times*, 13 Apr. 1971, p. 23.

40. Kovach, "Stolen Files."

41. "FBI Data Is Called Standard," *Delaware County Daily Times*, 12 Apr. 1971, p. 1.

42. Kovach, "Citizens Commission Writes to Seven Persons."

43. Charlene Canape, "FBI Data Released at PMC," *Delaware County Daily Times*, 22 Apr. 1971, p. 1.

44. Kitsi Burkhart and Paul F. Levy, "FBI Here Recruits Youth to Spy on New Left, Stolen Files Disclose," *Philadelphia Bulletin*, 21 Mar. 1971, p. 1.

45. Ibid.

46. Bill Kovach, "FBI File on War Foe Runs 5 Pages," *New York Times*, 25 Apr. 1971, p. 63.

47. William Greider, "Analysis of Stolen FBI Documents Provides Glimpse of Bureau at Work," *Washington Post*, 4 July 1971, p. A1.

48. Paul Cowan, Nick Egleson, and Nat Hentoff, *State Secrets: Police Surveillance in America* (New York: Holt, Rinehart & Winston, 1974), p. 116.

49. Bill Kovach, "Stolen FBI Papers Described as Largely of a Political Nature," *New York Times*, 13 May 1971, p. 18.

50. Ibid. The figures in the original documents also add up to 110%. See *The Complete Collection of Political Documents Ripped Off from the FBI Office in Media, PA, March 8, 1971* (Rifton, NY: WIN Peace and Freedom through Non-Violent Action, 1972).

51 Fred P. Graham, "Waiting for the Other Shoe to Drop," *New York Times*, 28 May 1971, p. 9.

52. FBI Memorandum, J. Edgar Hoover to Field Offices, 28 Apr. 1971.

53. FBI Memorandum, "The New Left Notes—Philadelphia," Philadelphia Special Agent-in-charge, 9. Sept. 1970; FBI memorandum, "COINTELPRO–New Left," Headquarters to Field Offices, 6 Sept. 1970.

54. Theodore H. White, *Breach of Faith: The Fall of Richard Nixon* (New York: Atheneum, 1975), p. 125.

2 The Communist Party U.S.A. COINTELPRO

I had no idea that the FBI was watching us or that an article on our church was being prepared for publication.

Dennis G. Kuby

At 10:00 A.M. on the morning of August 24, 1936, President Franklin D. Roosevelt held a private Oval Office meeting with FBI Director J. Edgar Hoover. The president, then in the final year of his first term, was becoming increasingly concerned about extremist political developments taking place in Europe and in Asia. FDR told Hoover he was quite worried that potentially hostile fascist and communist governments might have influence on extremist organizations, both right and left, in the United States.

It was a long meeting. As Hoover recalled, the president wanted "a broad picture of the general movement (of subversive activities) and its activities as (they) may affect the economic and political life of the country as a whole."[1]

The director confirmed the president's apprehensions by telling him that communist subversive elements within the United States were already planning to take over the powerful West Coast Longshoreman's Union, the United Mineworkers' Union, and other labor organizations.

In addition, Hoover said that there definitely were communist elements now within the U.S. government itself—particularly in the National Labor Relations Board. Lastly, Hoover alerted FDR to potential right-wing dangers.

The president, somewhat stunned, asked Hoover to set in motion immediately the machinery necessary to gather intelligence information on domestic communist and fascist organizations on a comprehensive and systematic basis. Hoover had to remind the president that, as much as he might want to begin surveillance on these subversive elements tomorrow, he could not. It was not illegal for a U.S. citizen to be a member of a communist or fascist organization. Technically, the FBI could not investigate.

However, as strange as it might seem, under its Appropriations Act the FBI was actually authorized to undertake investigations of this type at the request of the secretary of state—without going to the Congress. Roosevelt pondered the situation for a minute. Having to follow authorization procedures seemed like a terribly circuitous way to begin a major (albeit secret) investigation, particularly when, as he felt, the very security of the nation might be at stake. What the president wanted was an ultrasecret investigative program, since he would not go to Congress for funding or authorization. And the president was a pragmatist to his fingertips. He would just use the tools at his disposal! A White House meeting was set up for the next day, including Roosevelt, Hoover, and Secretary of State Cordell Hull.

The three men met the following afternoon at 1:00 P.M. in the White House. Their meeting did not take long. FDR turned to Secretary Hull and explained that he wanted the Federal Bureau of Investigation to begin a systematic survey of subversive activities in the country. This FBI operation was to be handled with the most extreme secrecy. In light of world developments, the program would, in all likelihood, be ongoing. Roosevelt paused and gathered his thoughts. He looked again at his secretary of state and said, "Edgar says he can do this but the request must come from you to make it legal." Hoover recalls that Hull said, "Go ahead and investigate the ——— thing!"[2]

Funding for the FBI investigation was then secretly allocated. The bureau was thus authorized to gather domestic intelligence, in this case, by presidential directive rather than by statute. No one in the legislative and judicial branches was informed. Almost no one in the executive branch besides the president knew. The attorney general—Hoover's nominal superior—was told only after the fact.

It is unlikely that any of the three men who met that day in the summer of 1936 imagined that their decision would be the first in a series of steps leading to a protracted expansion of domestic intelligence activities that eventually reached far beyond the investigation of criminal or subversive activities. In time, the FBI's operations would include not only the monitoring of political expression but, in many cases, the disruption of it. The seeds for the first COINTELPRO, which would come to fruition thirty years later, had been planted.

After the two White House meetings in August, Hoover moved quickly and with great skill and shrewdness. This was an optimum opportunity for the FBI to expand not only its role in serving the national interest, but also its size and power base—with virtually no hindrance whatever from anyone else in the government.

On September 10, at the president's request, Hoover briefed Attorney General Homer Cummings on the White House meetings. Later that month, instructions were issued to all FBI special agents nationwide: "Obtain from all possible sources information concerning subversive activities being conducted in the United States by communists, fascist representatives, or advocates of other organizations or groups advocating the overthrow of the Government of the United States by illegal methods."[3]

FBI officials moved into action.

A systematic file-classification system for managing intelligence information was put into use. A nationwide informant plan was designed and developed, aimed at penetrating to the core of subversive groups. A comprehensive reporting system was created almost overnight. The director would now receive daily briefings on major subversive developments whenever and wherever they occurred.

Additionally, as instructed by both the president and the attorney general, Hoover was to coordinate information with military intelligence officials and also with the State Department. The expanded area of responsibility came entirely under the bureau's newly formed General Intelligence Section. At the time the GIS was formed, Hoover reported that "this division now has compiled extensive indices of individuals, groups, and organizations engaged in these subversive activities, [and] in espionage activities or any activities that are possibly detrimental to the internal security of the United States.."[4] The exponential growth of the new section continued right up until the 1970s.

In 1938 at the request of the new attorney general, Frank Murphy, virtually all intelligence budgets were increased. Within this general increase, the expansion of internal-surveillance capabilities continued to remain, for all practical purposes, secret.

Some idea of the growth in size of the FBI in the late 1930s can be determined by noting that in 1938 the bureau, with a budget of $6.2 million, represented about 15 percent of the Justice Department's total budget; by 1940 the FBI budget had increased to $8.6 million, or 20 percent of the Justice Department budget.[5]

In fact, by 1939—with war becoming a distinct possibility for the United States—the FBI had become the paramount agency in the field of domestic intelligence operations.

In June 1939 Roosevelt issued a secret FBI directive confirming that the FBI had sole responsibility for coordination of the investigation of subversion anywhere in the United States. This June memo was the closest thing to a formal charter for FBI and military domestic intelligence operations that the American system would permit.[6] Another Roosevelt directive was issued in September 1939; it asked virtually all law enforcement officers in the United States to transmit to the FBI any and all information obtained by them in relation to sabotage, espionage, counterespionage, subversive, and similar activities.[7]

In keeping with the president's original intention, the wartime FBI counterintelligence programs were broad in scope and had two main purposes. The first was to supply the president and others in the executive branch with "pure intelligence"—the necessary intelligence data to make decisions and develop government policies. The second purpose was to compile preventive intelligence data for future use in actual war. The primary FBI targets for monitoring at this time were active communists and fascists.

The wartime performance of the FBI was, by any standard, excellent. The bureau was extraordinarily effective in combating foreign-inspired subversive activities. It investigated almost 20,000 cases of alleged sabotage, and dealt with many thousands of espionage complaints annually. Special agents proved quite capable in intercepting Japanese and German spy rings. The bureau played a major role in developing security plans for U.S. defense plants.

There was, however, another side to the FBI wartime story.

During the war, FBI domestic intelligence investigations went considerably beyond the investigation of actual crimes to include law-abiding organizations and individuals. The most intrusive and unregulated investigative techniques—justified perhaps by demanding wartime requirements—eventually opened the door for the COINTELPRO operations that would begin in the mid–1950s: electronic surveillance, mail openings, and surreptitious entry.

By 1945 the FBI annual budget had increased to almost $45 million, an increase of more than sevenfold since 1938. The FBI budget in 1945 was almost 43 percent that of the entire Justice Department.[8] This was the year the United States began reducing its massive military organization. The war was won. Germany, Italy, and Japan had been defeated. But the Soviet Union, wartime ally of the United States, almost immediately became the new enemy—the enemy in a "Cold War."

Hoover did not want to lose or squander the bureau's wartime growth in appropriations, size, scope, and authority. He *certainly* did not want to give up its newfound prestige. And—as was almost always the case—the director was not to be denied.

Prof. Tony Proveda has written, "It was a shrewd use of political intelligence and a massive public relations campaign to exploit cold war fears that eased the bureau's transition from wartime to peacetime and allowed it to maintain its wartime gains."[9] With its firsthand experience in monitoring the Communist party during the war, the FBI was in the unique position of being the nation's expert on the international and internal communist threat.

In 1945 the Communist Party U.S.A. (CPUSA) was at its highest membership count ever—between 75,000 and 85,000 members.[10] Of this total, about one-third were members of the Congress of Industrial Organizations (CIO) or were in unions either associated with or led by Communist party members. CPUSA consistently maintained a hard party line, in keeping with its concept of Soviet communism.

On March 7, 1946, Hoover advised Attorney General Tom C. Clark that the FBI was in the process of intensifying its investigation of the Communist party nationwide.[11] The bureau had programs in place to monitor areas directly identified with the Communist Party U.S.A., as well as those not directly identified but where party objectives were being promoted—organized labor; front organizations; racial, national, or political groups; and so forth. Instructions were issued to all FBI special agents to intensify their investigations of persons to be detained by the FBI in the event of a national emergency—those listed on the bureau's "Security Index." Later instructions called for the development of a new "Communist Index," which would be compiled in addition to the Security Index. This new index would include virtually all known Communist Party U.S.A. members anywhere.[12]

In 1947 President Truman reauthorized the bureau to conduct these investigations. Later that same year, in keeping with the rising tension of the Cold War, Truman approved the Loyalty and Security Program—a measure that would authorize government boards of inquiry to investigate the loyalty of federal employees.

The Loyalty and Security Program allowed for a very broad definition of the threat of subversive influence. It reinforced the secrecy of FBI informants, and it gave the bureau authority to conduct disloyalty investigations.

In 1950 the Emergency Detention Act became law. This act, which was drafted with the assistance of the secretary of defense and the attorney general, stipulated again that the FBI was the agency with authority to investigate any individual who might be detained in the event of a national emergency. Special attention would be given to key figures within the Communist party.

Also in 1950 the Congress passed—over President Truman's veto—the McCarran Act (the "Internal Security Act"), which established the Subversive Activities Control Board and specified that both communist-front and communist-action groups must register with the government.

Occasionally, the Justice Department would ask for reports from the FBI about its counterintelligence activities, which might not seem terribly unusual since the FBI is a part of the Department of Justice. But the Justice Department really knew very little about the true scope and depth of FBI counterintelligence activities. Certain programs, such as the Communist Index, were deliberately kept secret by the bureau. In other areas, such as the FBI programs aimed at "Marxist-type or other revolutionary groups not controlled by the Communist Party,"[13] the Justice Department was completely in the dark.

During this postwar period, the general confidence of the American public was shaken by a number of traumatic events: the matter of Alger Hiss, the Rosenberg spy case, the fall of China, the Korean War, the Soviet atomic bomb testing, the McCarthy hearings. The constant pronouncements made by J. Edgar Hoover to the effect that the Communist party was "a menace to the American way of life" did little to calm public fears.

By the time President Eisenhower took office in 1953, the FBI had completed checks on more than 6 million citizens for possible disloyalty. Twenty-five thousand Americans had been subjected to complete FBI field investigations. The bureau had employed about 1,600 special agents and 5,000 paid informants.[14] At this same time, in spite of its much larger work load, the FBI was continuing to operate in ever greater isolation from the rest of the Justice Department. There was a general sense in the country, and certainly in Congress, that whatever needed to be done about domestic communism should be done by the FBI. Exactly what the FBI was doing was all but unknown by anyone outside the bureau.

In any case, by 1956—less than ten years after its heyday—the Communist Party U.S.A. was in terrible shape. Forty-two indictments under the Smith Act were brought against it between 1953 and 1956. Antisubversion committees in both the House and Senate, together with deportation procedures against party members, had taken a heavy toll.

The FBI knew better than anyone else the true state of the Communist party. By 1956, membership had declined from its postwar high of 75,000–85,000 to only 22,000. The bureau also knew that the Communist Party U.S.A. was no longer being used by Soviet espionage, though it did represent a potential recruiting organization for subversive spies and recruits.

In 1956 the Supreme Court reduced the power of the government to investigate and prosecute those it deemed subversives under the authority of the Smith Act. The Smith Act, passed in 1940, made it a crime to advocate *in any way* "the overthrow of any government in the United States by force of violence."[15] In a new interpretation of the law, the Court held that simple advocacy of ideas was not, in and of itself, punishable. The government would now have to prove advocacy of actual violent actions in order to obtain convictions.

Hoover immediately announced that the ruling was a blow to the bureau's ability to fight subversion. The director had several things on his mind after the new Smith Act ruling. Over time, and during the numerous proceedings against the CPUSA, the covers of a number of FBI informants had been destroyed. This reduced the bureau's ability to infiltrate, no matter how enfeebled the party may have become. Hoover wanted to continue to take advantage of conflicts within the party, while at the same time applying pressure on the party as a whole so that it could not reorganize under another name.

And Hoover was to have his wish fulfilled.

At the 279th meeting of the National Security Council—which was held at the White House on March 8, 1956—Hoover received authorization for the extremely hard-hitting operations that came to be known by the acronym "COINTELPRO."

William L. Sullivan, former intelligence chief and assistant director of the FBI and one of the primary architects of COINTELPRO, was interviewed some years later, after he left the FBI. He was asked if Hoover had been sincere about the actual threat posed to the United States by the Communist party. Sullivan's reply was blunt and to the point: "No, of course he wasn't sincere. He knew the party didn't amount to a damn. But he used the party as an instrument to get appropriations from Congress."[16] John P. Mohr, former assistant to the director for administration of laws, noted, "Personally I think the party was practically brought to its knees."[17]

Stephen Springarn, a counterintelligence expert and former counsel for the Secret Service, took the FBI director even more severely to task by saying that "he [Hoover] was using scare tactics entirely as a drum beat in order to blow up his importance and appropriations, which was his perennial obsession."[18] Indeed, the Select Committee to Study Government Operations with respect to Intelligence Activities (the "Church Committee") went so far as to say that the FBI actually "impaired the democratic decision making process by its distorted intelligence reporting on Communist infiltration and influence on domestic political activity."[19]

Whether he felt so or not, however, Hoover continued to argue—as he had for twenty years—that the party threatened the very existence of the United States. Even though more than 1,500 FBI informants were already in operation against CPUSA, he insisted that vigilance must be maintained and even increased.

Hoover carried these intractable views with him to that National Security Council meeting on March 8, 1956. The audience gathered in the cabinet room included the president, the vice-president, the secretaries of state, defense, and treasury, plus the chairman of the Joint Chiefs of Staff and the directors of the CIA, the Budget Bureau, and the Atomic Energy Commission.

Hoover put on a virtuoso performance.

The title of his presentation was "The Present Menace of Communist Espionage and Subversion." The printed highlights of his talk, together with a number of carefully prepared charts and summaries, were distributed to the members of the council. He then reviewed in considerable detail his assessment of the current internal threat posed by the CPUSA. He discussed successful efforts against the party that were made possible by the provisions of the Smith Act, now weakened by the Supreme Court. The data presented by Hoover, we now know, made CPUSA appear far more menacing than it actually was. But since the FBI knew more about the party than anyone else in the government, there was no one in the council to question his thinking.

When Hoover had finished the formal part of his presentation, President Eisenhower wondered out loud how much of the information could be shared with the general public. In response, Hoover said that perhaps some of the information could be made available in the form of a general news release to the media.

The real reason for the director's presence that morning became apparent: The FBI wanted approval by the president and the council to use every means available to pursue and disrupt CPUSA. Hoover failed to mention that many of the means were already in use.

The president spoke again. Would the director explain what counterintelligence techniques he had in mind? The director was warming to the subject. "Sometimes," he said, "it is necessary to make a surreptitious entry where on occasion we have photographed secret communist records and other data of great use to our security." Additional counterintelligence methods were listed: safecracking; mail interception; telephone surveillance; microphone plants; trash inspection; infiltration, disorganization, and penetration of groups; falsely labeling group members as government informants; using informants to raise controversial issues within groups; encouraging the IRS to investigate target groups; encouraging street warfare between certain groups; using misinformation to disrupt target-group activities; mailing anonymous letters to target-group spouses in which allegations of infidelity are made; mailing reprints of controversial newspaper articles to encourage group disruption. In short, "every means available to secure information and evidence."

When Hoover finished, the cabinet room fell silent. No voice was raised in objection to any of the methods outlined by the director. Approval was thus secured at the highest level of the administration. For all practical purposes, no one outside of that room had any information about these operations. Former Attorney General Herbert Brownell— one of those in attendance on March 8, 1956—recalls, "The atmosphere at the meeting was that the FBI had given a good account of itself."[20]

Hoover next met with the FBI's fourteen top domestic intelligence experts to refine existing strategies and develop new methods to combat an already anemic Communist party.

In August 1956, instructions were sent from FBI headquarters in Washington to a number of field offices. Ultimately, twelve offices participated in COINTELPRO.

The main objectives were to capitalize on the prevailing turmoil within the party—caused by Khrushchev's denunciation of Stalin—and to prevent the merger of CPUSA and the Socialist Workers party (SWP). Also, the FBI targeted the National Committee to Abolish the House Un-American Activities Committee and various civil rights activists who were alleged to be under communist influence.

Commenting on this early period of COINTELPRO, J. Edgar Hoover said that it was a powerful program for the express purpose of disrupting, exposing, discrediting, and neutralizing the Communist Party U.S.A. and similar organizations and groups.[21]

About 40 percent of the actions involved sending anonymous, inflammatory material to target groups or to individuals within the target groups. The bureau would also make news announcements of derogatory information available to friendly media in order to expose the activities of target groups. Other times, selected investigative information (sometimes untrue) would be deliberately leaked to local media to reveal target-group activities. Agents would also advise local, state, and federal authorities of any civil and criminal violations by target-group members. In other situations, FBI special agents would notify target-group members' employers, prospective employers, and credit bureaus of their membership. In a number of instances, special agents even contacted target-group members to let them know that the FBI knew of their questionable activities—a particularly intimidating technique. Sometimes, fictitious organizations were created, complete with forged signatures and documents, membership cards, and so on—all to create and disrupt target groups. Pressure was brought to bear on colleges, universities, and other institutions to remove known communists from teaching positions and other positions of authority. The COINTELPRO techniques, primarily covert, had the main purpose of neutralizing targets.

From the beginning, in 1956, it was established that ideas submitted for COINTELPRO actions would originate from selected field offices, or from special agents attached to FBI headquarters in Washington. Selected field offices *had* to submit suggestions to headquarters for consideration on a regular basis. No COINTELPRO action could begin in the field without headquarters' knowing. In order to maintain administrative control as well as secrecy, every COINTELPRO document contained a warning to all special agents: "No counterintelligence action could be initiated by the field without specific bureau authorization."[22]

Each COINTELPRO proposal from the field would be routed to the Intelligence Division, and then to one of the seven section chiefs operating within the Intelligence Division. All the Communist party, Socialist Workers' party, and New Left programs (see Chapters 3 and 6 in addition to this chapter) were handled by the Internal Security Section; the White Hate Group COINTELPRO (see Chapter 4), by the Extremist Section; and the Black Nationalist Hate Group program (see Chapter 5), by the Racial Intelligence Section.

In most cases, the individual section chief would route the incoming field proposal to the COINTELPRO supervisor assigned to each of the programs. In all likelihood, the section chief would make no recommendations regarding the proposal; it was the program supervisor who made the initial decision to approve or disapprove the proposal. Following the supervisor's review (assuming it was favorable), the proposal would move up the ladder of authority. With the supervisor's recommendation attached, the proposal would be sent to the branch chief.

The branch chief would look at the proposal and, if it met with the chief's approval, it would be sent almost to the top—to Assistant Director William C. Sullivan in the Domestic Intelligence Division. Sullivan would then study the proposal and, in all probability, take it to the director for final approval.

It was Sullivan—working together with Hoover and a number of FBI branch chiefs—who actually ran the programs. And there are two other important facts to note about the COINTELPROs. First, approximately one-third of the COINTELPRO proposals were turned down. The majority of these denials came from the director's desk. And the primary reason for the director's denial of certain COINTELPROs concerned the public image of the bureau. Hoover would not allow the FBI to become involved in activities that might be exposed to the public, and thereby embarrass the FBI. Second, these programs existed—for all practical purposes—independently of the rest of the Justice Department. And even though the initial approval for COINTELPRO came from the White House, the programs came to exist independently of the attorneys general and the White House.

At the lower and middle levels of the Intelligence Division, the COINTELPROs were coordinated with all other activities taking place within the individual sections. The COINTELPROs received little target-selection input from headquarters. COINTELPRO was essentially a field-oriented program. There were some cases, however, where section chiefs did send out field directives instructing agents to intensify their efforts in particular areas. Field progress reports were submitted every ninety days to section chiefs.

Every individual along the way knew that Hoover was ultimately in charge. Thus, in every COINTELPRO, one must see the director's imprint.

The first COINTELPRO memorandum, dated May 18, 1956, came from Alan H. Belmont, the number-three man in the FBI. This memo instructed special agents in COINTELPRO-designated field offices to furnish FBI headquarters with the names of individuals who had been active in the Communist Party U.S.A. underground between 1951 and 1954.[23]

On August 28, 1956, another memo from Belmont acknowledged receipt of the requested CPUSA names. The memo noted that Communist party members "who are presently being covered by any technical or microphonic surveillance or other highly confidential investigation techniques where such disclosure might possibly jeopardize currently productive sources"[24] would be deleted. However, for those party members not under such sensitive observation, the Internal Revenue Service would be considered as a vehicle in the investigation.

It was known that certain CPUSA members had failed to file complete income-tax returns, or had filed their returns under an assumed name or failed to file returns at all.

Between 1956 and 1968, as part of its COINTELPRO operations against CPUSA, the FBI enjoyed unlimited informal access to IRS data. This enabled the FBI to identify contributors to organizations then under bureau surveillance. The FBI never told the Internal Revenue Service why they wanted selected returns; astonishingly, the IRS never asked.

However, in 1968 IRS officials at the highest levels discovered that the FBI was obtaining returns illegally—through informal contacts within the IRS. The bureau's method of obtaining returns was changed to conform with regulations.

Interestingly enough, even after the regulations were put into effect this aspect of COINTELPRO remained top secret. J. W. Yeagley, the Justice Department official who handled the FBI requests for returns after 1968, recalls that he personally had never heard of COINTELPRO and he had no idea what the tax returns were for.[25]

All told, the usage of tax returns in the COINTELPRO operations against the Communist Party U.S.A. was not terribly successful. During the entire existence of COINTELPRO, the FBI utilized tax returns in 130 cases.

In one of the few documented tax cases, a college professor at a Midwestern university was planning to attend the 1968 Democratic National Convention to be held in Chicago. This individual had been an FBI COINTELPRO target because of his radical political beliefs, and it was felt that he would probably be a disruptive element at the convention. Therefore, the FBI intended to initiate an IRS audit against him immediately before the convention. The special agent in charge of this FBI operation recalls the bureau's rationale in this instance: Any pressure that could be brought to bear on the professor could "only accrue to the benefit of the government and the general public."[26] In fact, the audit did not achieve the desired purpose of disrupting the professor's planning for a demonstration at the Democratic Convention. However, he did experience an additional tax burden of $500.

Communist party attempts to infiltrate organizations were consistently neutralized by the bureau. FBI agents nearly always knew in advance what groups the Communist party targeted for infiltration—targets as diverse in membership as the National Association for the Advancement of Colored People (NAACP) and the United Farm Workers. When a Communist party member infiltrated an organization, an FBI agent usually approached the organization's leader with the startling information that a known communist had joined. In most cases this was disruptive enough to eliminate potential subversive activity.

The first COINTELPRO document that specifically mentioned the danger of Communist party infiltration of black groups was a memo mailed to COINTELPRO-approved field offices on October 2, 1956. It was written by Hoover, and it discussed the political resolutions adopted at a major CPUSA conference held in September 1956. Hoover laid out the strategy to be used by the bureau to infiltrate and disrupt CPUSA, together with instructions on developing and working with party informants. The memo also reminded special agents that informants would vary from place to place and that "the Negro situation is a paramount issue in the South."[27]

A few years later, a COINTELPRO memo—dated May 24, 1960—was mailed to the director from the New Haven, Connecticut, field office.

As shown below, it discussed the fact that a member of the Communist Party U.S.A. had succeeded in being elected to various executive positions within the local chapter of the NAACP. A follow-up strategy was proposed in which "concerned" letters would be mailed to the Hartford Chapter of the NAACP as a disruptive technique.

UNITED STATES GOVERNMENT
MEMORANDUM

TO: DIRECTOR, FBI (100–3–104)   DATE: May 24, 1960
FROM: SAC, NEW HAVEN (100–
           16559)
SUBJECT: COMMUNIST PARTY, USA
           COUNTERINTELLIGENCE
           PROGRAM
           INTERNAL SECURITY—C

ReBulet to New York dated 3/31/60. Reference is further made to Bufile [deleted] on [deleted].
It may be noted that [deleted], who has a rather extensive history of Communist Party activity, has been successful on two occasions in getting elected [deleted] of the New Haven Chapter of the NAACP, and occupies that position at the present time.
The Bureau is requested to authorize the New Haven office
to anonymously mail the enclosed letter to [deleted], National Association for the Advancement of Colored People, Hartford, Connecticut.
A search of the indices of the New Haven Office developed no derogatory information identifiable with [deleted].
2—Bureau (Enc.2) (RM)
1—New Haven
TS:md
(3)

                                        (Current date)
                                        New Haven, Conn.

    [deleted]
    [deleted]
    [deleted]
    National Association for the Advancement of Colored People
    Hartford, Connecticut

Dear Sir:

I am writing you this letter as a member of the New Haven Chapter of the National Association for the Advancement of Colored People, being greatly concerned over the fact that [deleted] continues to hold a position of local leadership in our organization.

Although [deleted]'s "leftist" views were long known to all of us who were well acquainted with him, he came to public attention through newspaper publicity during hearings before the House Un-American Activities Committee held in New Haven in [deleted].

Following the reelection in [deleted] of the local Chapter of our organization, I decided to inquire further into his Communist background. With this thought in mind I wrote to the Government Printing Office in Washington, D.C., for a copy of the Hearings before the Committee on Un-American Activities held in New Haven in [deleted]. As a result of this request I was sent Part I of the report on Investigation of Communist Activities in the New Haven, Conn., area.

On page 5607 of that report there is contained the account of testimony of [deleted] who was being questioned by Staff Member [deleted]. The following is a partial quotation from the testimony of [deleted]:

[deleted]. Now kindly tell us, if you please sir, who were the members of the Negro Commission of the Communist Party with which you were identified.

[deleted]. Well, I can give you a list of the members, sir. After a certain period of time it was reduced because of the problem of meeting in security.

[deleted]. All right, sir.

[deleted]. There was [deleted] from New Haven, I think his first name was [deleted].

While the above appears to be the most serious allegation made against [deleted], there were other references made during the course of this hearing concerning his subversive connections. If this much information could be obtained by me, a private citizen, with a minimum amount of effort on my part, think how much more might be developed by a complete investigation. In these days when we are engaged in an all important struggle for equality for members of our race, can we afford to continue to offer our enemies such a justifiable basis for criticizing our organization?

If [deleted] is to be removed from leadership in our organization without unnecessary embarrassment to our group, it must be accomplished as a self-imposed "house-cleaning" operation, and not following his exposure by our enemies.

It is earnestly suggested that you use the influence of your office to initiate this "house-cleaning" operation before it is too late.

Very truly yours[28]

The explosive FBI letter evidently missed its target completely, however, or possibly the target didn't exist in the first place. Perhaps it was a figment of the FBI's sometimes rather bizarre imagination.

Edwin Edmonds, a minister of the United Church of Christ in New Haven, has been an active member in the NAACP for more than thirty years. "In 1960," Reverend Edmonds recalls, "there were four or five board members in the New Haven Chapter. I knew them all well. We were card carrying NAACP members but certainly not card carrying communists! We were still feeling some of the effects of McCarthyism and, of course, Martin Luther King was already publicly active in the civil rights struggle. We were awfully busy. None of us had the slightest notion about being involved with communists, I can't imagine what the FBI was thinking. I'm sure that the letter was thrown away in less than five minutes. We had more important things to do!"[29]

In another action, which took place in July 1961, the FBI reprinted an anticommunist article written by an African student who had attended college in the Soviet Union. The article, entitled "I Was a Student at Moscow State University," originally appeared in the July 1961 *Reader's Digest*. It discussed the intense discrimination that the black student encountered there. The FBI mailed the article anonymously to prominent black leaders throughout the United States. The intended message was obvious: Life under communist rule was no bed of roses for blacks.

Hoover, as he said in countless memos, always felt the CPUSA would focus its full attention on this group—one of America's most deprived minorities—since blacks made up 10 percent of the nation's population. In January 1961 Hoover acted on this concern by sending a memorandum to members of the new Kennedy administration. This memo, addressed to Robert F. Kennedy, Byron White, and Dean Rusk, outlined the communist threat as he viewed it from the director's chair.

Hoover discussed CPUSA COINTELPRO operations and noted that the program was intended to keep "CPUSA off balance with reference to the questions of Communist Party infiltration of black organizations."[30] The director also mentioned that during 1959 the FBI was able to prevent CPUSA from seizing control of the 20,000-member branch of the National Association for the Advancement of Colored People in Chicago.

J. Edgar Hoover's obsessive and largely unwarranted concern about CPUSA's infiltration of black political organizations led to one of the most shameful episodes in American civil rights history: the prolonged investigation of the most charismatic of all the black leaders, Dr. Martin Luther King, Jr.

The King investigation began under the auspices of the CPUSA COINTELPRO and, by the late 1960s, was moved to the Black Hate COINTELPRO. FBI surveillance of King began in 1957. As King's civil rights activities expanded throughout the nation, the FBI assigned more special agents to monitor and, when possible, disrupt the movement. CPUSA COINTELPRO expansions to cover black activities occurred in 1960 and 1963. Indeed, by the end of 1963 the FBI was monitoring the Congress of Racial Equality (CORE), the Student Non-violent Coordinating Committee (SNCC), the NAACP, and a number of other groups.

Martin Luther King was, however, the chief focus of the FBI. In January 1963 Hoover flatly asserted in several memos that King was associating with communists. By the spring of that year the FBI officially listed King as a communist in the FBI Reserve Index. In the event of a national emergency, King was to be detained.

The civil rights movement gained force through the spring and early summer of 1963. It was at this time that the watershed event of American civil rights history—the March on Washington—was being planned.

Hoover sent a blizzard of memos to the Justice Department. One of his missives written at the time asserts that "the party is actively supporting the march," and that "all offices will remain alert for future possible situations involving the Negro and the party."[31] Another document reports that "the party is making an all out effort to take advantage of this opportunity [the march] to further its cause."[32] On July 29, just twenty-nine days before the event, Hoover sent out a report prepared by the New York field office that was entitled "Martin Luther King, Jr.—Affiliation with the Communist Movement." A file called "Communist Influence in Racial Matters" was also opened.[33]

In spite of Hoover's assertion that more than 200 Communist party members attended the march,[34] there was not much real cause for alarm. The March on Washington—the largest public demonstration ever held in the nation's capital—was the very model of a peaceful protest. If there were 200 party members there (which is doubtful), their ranks were certainly dissipated by the crowd of more than 200,000.

Later in recalling the march, William C. Sullivan—one of the bureau architects of the program to monitor Martin Luther King—said in his usual colorful style that "Hoover had some damn thing in mind where he wanted to smear the American Negro as being pro-communist. . . . Well, hell, the Negro never infiltrated the Communist Party.[35]

Nevertheless, on October 1, 1963, Hoover approved a special COMINFIL (communist infiltration) COINTELPRO plan of action that directed an intensified "coverage of communist influence on the Negroes."[36] A COMINFIL investigation is generally utilized when there is evidence that the party has specifically instructed its members to infiltrate an organization—in this case, supposedly, the Southern Christian Leadership Conference (SCLC).

Martin Luther King, as the nation's most prominent black spokesman, would receive the full FBI counterintelligence broadside. Almost every weapon in the FBI's COINTELPRO arsenal was brought into use. In October 1963, Attorney General Robert F. Kennedy—after a great deal of personal hesitation—approved the use of wiretaps against King. Hidden-microphone surveillance was also undertaken by the FBI—without the approval of the attorney general. These aggressive surveillance techniques were used for almost two years.

As the FBI was authorized to do "in matters of national security," the King surveillance expanded to include taps at the King home, the headquarters of the Southern Christian Leadership Conference in both Atlanta and New York, and motel rooms in Los Angeles, Atlantic City, Washington, D.C., Milwaukee, Honolulu, Detroit, Sacramento, and Savannah.

The surveillance was originally authorized for the express purpose of determining the extent, if any, of CPUSA involvement with King and the civil rights movement. However, the FBI also used information found through surveillance to launch personally degrading attacks on King, with the purpose of discrediting him.

Arthur Murtagh, former FBI agent at the Atlanta office, remembers that "5,000 of King's calls were intercepted over a period of years. . . . The surveillance was massive and complete. He couldn't wiggle."[37]

The King surveillance revealed nothing about national security. There was no information about or evidence of communist infiltration of the movement.

There was, however, information of a different nature. The tapes revealed information about King's alleged sexual "extracurricular activities."

One of the most astonishing episodes in the whole sordid King–FBI COINTELPRO affair took place in November 1964.

A composite tape was made of recordings taken at hotel rooms in Los Angeles, San Francisco, and Washington, D.C. The FBI laboratory in Washington "sanitized" the finished tape—which meant it could not be easily traced back to the FBI. The plan originally was to mail the tape to Mrs. King.

Instead, the tape was given to a special agent who took it to Miami and mailed it directly to King himself from a post office near the Miami airport. Accompanying the tape was a letter. It implied that if King would end his own life the tape would not be made public.

In interviews years later, Mrs. King recalled receiving the tape and noted, "Martin and I listened to the tape and we found much of it unintelligible. We concluded that there was nothing in the tape to discredit him."[38]

As threatened, the tape was made available to various media personnel, but not a one was interested.

Summaries of the wiretap surveillance information were sent to President Johnson and the attorney general, in hopes of discrediting King at the White House.

And in January 1964 Director Hoover implied, in off-the-record comments before the House Appropriations Committee, that King was associating with communists and also that King's personal life was highly unsavory. Testimony like this did not remain secret for long in the Congress.

Also in early 1964 it was learned that King had been selected to receive honorary degrees from Marquette University and Springfield College. The FBI attempted to have both institutions withdraw their invitations. One did and one did not.

Later that same year the FBI contacted the general secretary of the National Council of the Churches of Christ in an attempt to persuade the organization to withhold financial support from the SCLC. After meeting with Sullivan, the secretary stated, "Martin Luther King will never get 'one single dollar' of financial support from the National Council."[39]

Again in 1964 the bureau learned that King was planning to visit the pope, and it tried to have the audience canceled. The FBI felt that the meeting would certainly enhance the civil rights leader's prestige both in the United States and abroad.

Assistant Director Malone of the New York bureau office met with

Francis Cardinal Spellman, and Malone reported that "the Cardinal took instant steps to advise the Vatican against granting any audience to King. . . . Cardinal Spellman is going to Rome next week . . . and thus will be on the scene personally and further insure that the Pope is not placed in an embarrassing position through any contact with King."[40]

These FBI efforts were, however, unsuccessful. The pope did meet with King. The bureau also tried—against unsuccessfully—to discredit King during his receipt of the Nobel Peace Prize.

Perhaps the most telling statement about the investigation and why the bureau pursued King so vengefully was expressed in a COINTEL-PRO document dated March 4, 1968, just one month before King was slain. One of the COINTELPRO goals, it stated, was to "prevent the rise of a messiah who could unify and electrify the militant black nationalist movement."[41]

William C. Sullivan appeared before the Church Committee several years later. He testified, with specific reference to the King investigation, that "he never heard anyone raise the question of legality or constitutionality, never."[42]

Active CPUSA COINTELPRO operations were not limited to concerns about communist penetration of the civil rights movement. In a 1960 case involving the Detroit field office, the FBI made anonymous calls to the editors of three local newspapers asserting that an upcoming speech at a nearby university was being sponsored by a communist-front organization. The purpose of the FBI calls was to prevent a communist-sponsored speaker from appearing on campus. Because of various pressures, the university decided to cancel the speech. However, the university did call the Detroit field office for more detailed information on the allegedly communist speaker. The university administration was told that this type of information was confidential and could not be revealed.

The speech was canceled. The American Civil Liberties Union (ACLU) became interested in the case though, and took the matter to court. It was decided that the university could not ban the speaker from his campus appearance. The FBI then began a fruitless investigation of the judge.

In the Washington, D.C., area the bureau moved to discredit a local couple long identified with the Communist Party U.S.A. The FBI furnished news media in Washington with the information that the couple's son had, in fact, been arrested on drug charges. The FBI news release also noted that "the Russian born mother is currently under a deportation order" and that she was married to a prominent Communist party member.[43]

The Cleveland field office, working with information supplied by a confidential source, developed a news release about a local Unitarian church. It asserted that the Unitarian Society of Cleveland was backing efforts to abolish the House Committee on Un-American Activities, and the news piece was anonymously mailed to the *Cleveland Times*, a local conservative weekly. The paper picked up the story immediately and ran it with the somewhat hysterical headline "LOCALS TO AID RED LINE." The article went on to name the Unitarian minister, Reverend Dennis G. Kuby, and several church members as instruments in a plot to terminate the House Committee.

Reverend Kuby remembers well the day the FBI article appeared in the *Cleveland Times*. "I was completely thunderstruck," he recalls. "I had no idea that the FBI was watching us or that an article on our church was being prepared for publication." The Unitarian Society parish members were generally well educated and tended to be liberal. Kuby was a supporter of Martin Luther King.

Reverend Kuby, now the director of a ministry in Berkeley, California, realizes that "there must have been an FBI infiltration of the parish itself, although I had no direct contact with the FBI. Our stand on the House Committee on Un-American Activities was certainly our right. The FBI was undermining the Constitution it was seeking to protect. They were completely out of line."

For about a year after the article appeared, Kuby and other church members received considerable abuse—crank telephone calls, hate mail, a hostile reception on a television talk show. And it seems certain that Kuby's phone was tapped.

"If I had it to do all over again I would take the same stand on the same issues," Kuby says.[44]

Another incident—quite serious at the time—now seems rather amusing.

A Communist party official planned to hold a secret two-week training seminar for area youths in a Midwestern city in 1967. The FBI, however, arranged it so he would be greeted on his arrival at the local airport by—of all people—a news reporter and film crew. The communist quite simply blew his top, angrily pushed the reporter away, and swung his briefcase at the film crew as it was shooting the entire melee. The incident was, of course, featured live on local television news broadcasts. So much for the secrecy of that training program.

In 1968 the Phoenix field office targeted a college professor who had been deeply involved with a local antiwar center. The professor had recently resigned in order to head the McCarthy for President campaign in the Phoenix area. The FBI, however, felt that in good time the professor would find his way back to the peace center. After diligent investigation, the bureau discovered that the professor in question was married to a member of the Communist Party U.S.A. The FBI jumped on this information with both feet. The finding, together with a variety of sordid details, was supplied to a local paper. The newspaper ran the article in due course, with the peace-center group labeled as "professional revolutionaries."[45]

The New York field office became interested in the bizarre situation of a wealthy real estate investor, recently deceased, who had left more than $1 million to the Communist Party U.S.A.. Special agents interviewed the probate judge involved with the case, and found him to be cooperative. The judge advised the agents to interview the man's widow to see if she would contest the will in order to keep the funds out of the hands of the Communist party.

In addition, the FBI contacted a probate attorney, seeking advice on how the will could be contested; agents contacted other relatives of the deceased, asked for advice from the Internal Revenue Service and state taxing authorities, and also leaked information about the content of the will to a New York newspaper. However, all the bureau's efforts to gain any help in contesting the will proved unsuccessful.

Other COINTELPRO harassments of the CPUSA included working to produce hostility between the Communist Party U.S.A. and the Socialist Workers party by way of anonymous and acrimonious telephone calls and letters; providing information to news reporters about the participation of CPUSA presidential candidate, Bettina Aptheken, in the United Farm Workers' picket lines; and linking a school boycott in San Francisco with the Communist party by informing the media that the boycott leader planned to attend a special reception at the Soviet mission.

Schoolteachers became special COINTELPRO targets because of their unique position of influence over the thinking of young people. One high school teacher became a direct COINTELPRO target because he had invited radical antidraft speakers to the school. The FBI sent anonymous letters about the teacher's choice of speakers to local newspapers, the board of education, and the school's administration office.

Other techniques resembling what came to be called, in post-Watergate parlance, "dirty tricks" included packing Communist party rallies and meetings with vocal and obnoxious anticommunists, sending invitations to Communist party functions that would never take place, provoking last-minute cancellations of rental halls for party functions, and providing reporters with hostile questions for communists they planned to interview.

The Los Angeles field office, working through a carefully developed friendly media contact, was able to have several feature articles placed in the *Los Angeles Examiner* and the *Los Angeles Herald Express* in October 1961. These articles called attention to a "freedom of the press" banquet being attended by more than 1,000 persons in the area. Speakers with communist backgrounds were in attendance. Prof. Dirk J. Struck of the Massachusetts Institute of Technology, the featured speaker, was described as a man with a Marxist background. Editorially, the *Examiner* noted that "there is little difference, if any, between the Nazi–Fascist block then, and the objectives of Marxism today." The bureau follow-up memorandum said that these editorials "and articles were extremely effective in alerting the public to the communist nature at the banquet."[46]

The Milwaukee field office became involved in a COINTELPRO action against the den mother of a local Cub Scout troop.

The FBI learned of her communist connection through informants in 1962. In its initial salvo, the FBI—again working through friendly media contacts—was successful in placing with a major local newspaper an article explaining that Mary Blair was married to a prominent communist and that she was also involved with the Cub Scouts.

Next the FBI contacted Ms. Blair's employer, the Olson Publishing Company, in an effort to have her fired. Despite repeated bureau contacts, the publisher refused to relieve Blair of her job. The FBI was not to be denied. Somehow, bureau agents obtained the names and addresses of every employee of Olson Publishing, each of whom received in the mail a complete rundown of information on Mary Blair. After a fight of more than a year, the employer finally relented and fired her. Blair, however, won out in the end: She brought an action for damages against the FBI and was awarded almost $50,000 in a court settlement.[47]

One of the most protracted single episodes in the COINTELPRO story concerned the "snitch jacket" operation against William Albertson, a member of the Communist party ruling elite—the National Committee. Albertson was a lifelong Communist and had been convicted on Smith Act charges.

In 1964 a document that implicated Albertson as an FBI informant was found by a party member in a car in which Albertson had been a passenger. The document had been prepared and planted by the FBI.

To Communist party officials, however, the document seemed genuine; and Albertson was immediately expelled from the party. Thus, he was hit from both sides. The FBI had implicated him as one of its informants, while it continued to investigate him as if he were still a party member in good standing. Even after the frame-up was made public, the party refused to accept Albertson back in good standing.

Over a period of many months, Albertson and his wife were the subjects of crank calls and personal harassment tactics. They were forced to change jobs and to move. The FBI even attempted to influence a Supreme Court case in which William Albertson was involved.

Incredibly, the FBI and the IRS later approached him and asked if he would work as an informant against the party that had expelled him. Albertson refused. He protested his innocence to the party all during the bureau investigation, which lasted for five years.

His wife described him as a "broken man" at his death in 1972.

After the success of this operation in which an activist had been made to seem an informant, the bureau decided that this was "a most unique and sensitive counterintelligence technique."[48]

In many cases, the special agents who did the actual legwork of the COINTELPRO operations became disenchanted with their assignments—sometimes very quickly. Bob Wall, a former special agent in the Washington field office, noted that there was an absolute obsession with communism within the bureau, though few outside the bureau shared its overwhelming concern. The reason for the FBI's obsession was that Hoover himself was obsessed with communism. Much of his concern had little basis in reality.

Special Agent Wall remembers an assignment to monitor street demonstrations in Washington, D.C., by photographing participants, taking down license numbers, and recording the speeches. Wall remembers realizing that there simply wasn't much of a communist threat. He remembers asking one of his superiors, "Why are we covering this demonstration?" He was told that the communists were attempting to infiltrate the peace movement and the civil rights movement. The FBI was to find the hidden communists and protect America. This, of course, was chapter and verse what Hoover would have said. It was not acceptable to monitor large demonstrations and come back with a report on only one person who, according to bureau records, was a communist. Rather, agents were instructed to bring back as many photographs and license numbers as humanly possible. With more names to process, the special agents would then have quite a number of investigative files to open. Higher numbers of investigative files impressed congressional committees. Wall remembers preparing mountains of paperwork on people whose most radical view was wishing an end to the Vietnam War.

Special Agent Wall recalls that in 1967 the Communist Party U.S.A. had exactly three active members in Washington, D.C. However, it was a COINTELPRO function also to keep track of individuals who had *once* been active party members. Such an operation tended to develop a life of its own. Data would be updated by special agents once, twice, three, four times a year. This meant that each individual case had to be reopened, reassigned, and closed. Then the whole procedure would have to be started all over again the next year—a task that must have seemed as futile as Sisyphus rolling his stone.

After five years as a special agent, Wall decided to end his FBI career. He remembers beginning to loathe himself for the type of COINTELPRO work he was doing. Agent Wall announced that he could no longer accept the policy directives offered by the FBI.[49]

One of the most widely used weapons in the COINTELPRO arsenal was the paid undercover informant, used in about 85 percent of domestic intelligence investigations. More than 1,500 informants were used in the Communist Party U.S.A. COINTELPRO.

In this context, the story of William T. Divale, who in 1965 was a twenty-three-year-old student at Pasadena City College, is interesting. Divale was originally approached by Wayne Shaw, then the special agent in charge of the Pasadena suboffice, to do undercover work within the Communist Party U.S.A.

The idea of undercover assignments appealed to the young student. He signed a security clearance with the FBI and was sworn to secrecy. He would be known within the bureau as a "subcontractor," not as an employee of the FBI. He was assigned a code name and paid on a monthly basis in cash.

Divale describes in considerable detail how, as an FBI undercover operator in southern California, he worked to gain actual membership in the Communist party—starting at the bottom and then moving up rather quickly through the various chains of command.

Divale was required to attend party meetings or lectures almost every night in Los Angeles. Soon he became chairman of the Los Angeles W.E.B. Du Bois Club. At this point, he passed on the entire membership roster of the local Du Bois Club (about 3,000 names) to the FBI. Divale penetrated other protest movements and reported his findings to the FBI on a regular basis. He was also used to "check out" certain professors at Cal Tech. Generally, over a period of years, Divale would meet with his bureau contacts in FBI sedans. At other times, his written reports to his FBI handler would simply be left in a government car. Elaborate measures were taken to determine if he and the FBI were being followed by CPUSA. As time progressed, Divale began to notice his own surveillance photography showing up in FBI files—a curious feeling.

As an undercover agent Divale crossed and crisscrossed the country in an attempt to get a national perspective on CPUSA. He participated in "teach-ins" and demonstrations, attended CPUSA conventions, marched in Washington, D.C., and attended Marxist retreats—all the while sending written reports to the FBI.

Divale estimates that he submitted more than 800 reports to the FBI during his time as an undercover agent, and named thousands of names. He earned more money being a spy for the FBI against the CPUSA than as an officer for CPUSA itself.

Divale—now an instructor at an Eastern university—recalls that, ultimately, he became profoundly disillusioned. "I'd been wrong in working for the bureau. It was morally corrupting for the FBI or any government agency to recruit one citizen to spy against another. It corrupted all citizens. . . . I stood as a tawdry symbol of that corruption. For none had been more corrupted than I."[50]

The Communist Party U.S.A. COINTELPRO was brought to a halt by the shattering trauma of the Media, Pennsylvania, office robbery. Hoover feared additional exposure of the bureau's secret counterintelligence programs and ordered that all programs be cancelled. Thus, on April 28, 1971, a headquarters memo ordered that "effective immediately, all COINTELPROs operated by this bureau are discontinued."[51]

The COINTELPRO effort against CPUSA had indeed been prodigious. Over a fourteen-year period there had been 1,850 separate action proposals submitted by field offices; 1,388 were approved, with known results achieved in 222 situations.

But was the operation worthwhile or really necessary? Probably not.

One researcher has suggested that "the Communist Party was a push-over for the FBI."[52] This is true. The party had approximately 22,000 members when COINTELPRO began in 1956. By 1971 the figure was down to about 3,000 members, with many being inactive and others being FBI informants.[53]

The FBI had so infiltrated the ranks of the CPUSA that agents and informants could actually make party policy.

The First and Fourth Amendment violations during the project had been considerable. The costs in human anxiety had been immense. And the reasons to fear the CPUSA were, of course, vastly overstated by Hoover. The Communist Party U.S.A. was a paper tiger.

NOTES

1. Senate Select Committee to Study Governmental Operations with Respect to Intelligence Activities, "Intelligence Activities and the Rights of Americans," Book II, 94th Cong., 2d sess., 14 Apr. 1976, quote from FBI Memorandum by J. Edgar Hoover, 24 Aug. 1936, at p. 25.

2. Ibid.

3. Senate Select Committee, "Intelligence Activities and the Rights of Americans," Book II, pp. 24–28.

4. Frank J. Donner, *The Age of Surveillance* (New York: Alfred A. Knopf, 1980), p. 59.

5. Tony G. Proveda, "FBI and Domestic Intelligence," *Journal of Crime and Delinquency* (April 1982): 197.

6. Senate Select Committee, "Intelligence Activities and the Rights of Americans," Book II, see Confidential Memorandum of the President, 1939, at p. 27.

7. Senate Select Committee, "Intelligence Activities and the Rights of Americans," Book II, p. 27.

8. Ibid.

9. Proveda, "FBI and Domestic Intelligence," pp. 194–210.

10. David A. Shannon, *The Decline of American Communism* (Chatham, N.J.: Chatham Bookseller, 1959), p. 3.

11. FBI Memorandum, J. Edgar Hoover to Attorney General Tom C. Clark, 8 Mar. 1946.

12. FBI Memorandum, FBI Headquarters to Field Offices, 15 Mar. 1948; Special Agents-in-charge letter, No. 57, Ser. 1948, 10 Apr. 1948.

13. FBI Memorandum, F. J. Baumgardner to A. H. Belmont, 8 June 1951.

14. Morton H. Halperin, Jerry J. Erman, Robert L. Borosage, and

Christine M. Marwick, *The Lawless State: The Crimes of U.S. Intelligence Agencies* (New York: Penguin Books, 1976).

15. Sanford J. Unger, *FBI: An Uncensored Look behind the Walls* (Boston: Little, Brown, 1975), p. 131.

16. Ovid Demaris, *The Director: An Oral Biography of J. Edgar Hoover* (New York: Harper's Magazine Press, 1975), p. 167.

17. Ibid.

18. Ibid., p. 123.

19. Senate Select Committee, "Intelligence Activities and the Rights of Americans," Book II, p. 82.

20. Minutes of the 279th Meeting of the National Security Council, Cabinet Room of the White House, 8 Mar. 1956, 9:00 A.M.; Herbert Brownell, testimony before U.S. District Court, Southern District of New York, June 2, 1981.

21. Senate Select Committee, "Intelligence Activities and the Rights of Americans," Book II, pp. 65–67.

22. House Committee on the Judiciary, Civil Rights and Constitutional Rights Subcommittee, *Hearings on FBI Counterintelligence Programs*, 93rd Cong., 2d sess., 20 Nov. 1974, Serial No. 55, p. 12.

23. FBI Memorandum, Alan H. Belmont to Special Agents, 18 May 1956.

24. FBI Memorandum, Alan H. Belmont to L. V. Boardman, 28 Aug. 1956.

25. Senate Select Committee, "Intelligence Activities and the Rights of Americans," Book II, p. 853; Statement of J. W. Yeagley to Senate Select Committee, Sept. 1975.

26. FBI Memorandum, Midwest City Field Office to FBI Headquarters, 1 Aug. 1968.

27. FBI Memorandum, J. Edgar Hoover to Special Agent-in-charge, New York Field Office, 2 October 1956.

28. FBI Memorandum, Special Agent-in-charge, New Haven Field Office, to J. Edgar Hoover, 24 May 1960. All deletions noted throughout this book were made by the FBI at the time that their records were made public. See Chapter 7.

29. Rev. Edwin Edmonds, United Church of Christ, New Haven, Conn., telephone interview with author, 22 July 1989.

30. FBI Memoranda File, "Communist Party U.S.A.—Negro Question," 23 August 1963, pp. 1–49.

31. FBI Memorandum, J. Edgar Hoover to Field Offices, July 1963.

32. FBI Memorandum, F. J. Baumgardner to W. C. Sullivan, 23 Aug. 1963.

33. Report of Special Agent, "Martin Luther King, Jr.—Affiliation with the Communist Movement," 22 July 1963; FBI Memorandum, Courtney

Evans to Alan H. Belmont, 29 July 1963; FBI Memorandum, Headquarters to Field Offices, 18 July 1963.

34. FBI Memorandum, J. Edgar Hoover to All Special Agents-in-charge, 24 Sept. 1963.

35. Demaris, *The Director*, p. 201.

36. FBI Memorandum, J. Edgar Hoover to Special Agents-in-charge, 1 Oct. 1963.

37. Paul Cowan, Nick Egleson, and Nat Hentoff, *State Secrets: Police Surveillance in America* (New York: Holt, Rinehart & Winston, 1974), p. 39.

38. Nicholas M. Horrock, "Ex-officials Say FBI Harassed Dr. King to Stop His Criticism," *New York Times*, 9 Mar. 1975, p. 40.

39. FBI Memorandum, W. C. Sullivan to Alan H. Belmont, 16 Dec. 1964.

40. FBI Memorandum, F. J. Baumgardner to W. C. Sullivan, 8 Sept. 1964.

41. FBI Memorandum, Headquarters to Field Offices, 4 Mar. 1968.

42. Statement of W. C. Sullivan to Senate Select Committee, 1 Nov. 1975.

43. FBI Memorandum, F. J. Baumgardner to W. C. Sullivan, 3 June 1963.

44. Rev. Dennis G. Kuby, Ministry of Ecology, Berkeley, California, telephone interview with author, 10 July 1989; FBI Memorandum, Cleveland Field Office to Headquarters, 6 Nov. 1964.

45. Senate Select Committee, "Intelligence Activities and the Rights of Americans," Book II, p. 61.

46. FBI Memorandum, W. C. Sullivan to F. J. Baumgardner, 23 Oct. 1961.

47. Donner, *Age of Surveillance*, pp. 186–87.

48. FBI Memoranda File, 1962–1967, FBI Albertson, "Snitch Jacket," Center for National Security Studies I–43, Washington, D.C.

49. Neil J. Welch and David W. Marston, *Inside Hoover's FBI* (Garden City, N.Y.: Doubleday, 1984).

50. William Tulio Divale with James Joseph, *I Lived inside the Campus Revolution* (New York: Coles Book, 1972), p. 198.

51. FBI Memorandum, J. Edgar Hoover to Special Agents-in-charge, 28 Apr. 1971.

52. Unger, *FBI: An Uncensored Look*, p. 124.

53. Unger, *FBI: An Uncensored Look*.

3 The Socialist Workers Party COINTELPRO

A disruptive program along similar lines [to that against CPUSA] could be initiated against the SWP on a very selective basis.

J. Edgar Hoover

The Socialist Workers party first came under FBI scrutiny in 1940. Members of the SWP saw themselves as followers of the principles of Marx, Engels, Lenin, and Trotsky, with the emphasis on interpretations of Trotsky.

Rhetorically, the SWP tended to project itself as part of a worldwide network that might advocate violence directed toward the U.S. government, should certain conditions arise within the United States. Its verbal support of such extreme causes as the Irish Republican Army, the Palestine Liberation Organization, and the Fair Play for Cuba Committee did not go unnoticed by the FBI.

It is probably safe to say that the ultimate goal of the SWP was the abolition of capitalism in the United States. Such a monumental change would be accomplished through the creation of a republic for farmers and workers, probably occurring through a lengthy historical process.

The ultimate objective was a simple one. The working-class majority would be in authority.

With many of these considerations in mind, the first FBI memo concerning SWP was written by J. Edgar Hoover in 1941. It directed that certain political groups, including the Socialist Workers party, would be investigated under the government's Custodial Detention Program.

Late in 1941, in what came to be known as the Dunne case, eighteen SWP members were prosecuted by the Justice Department for violation of the Smith Act. In this case the government said that a group of SWP members had openly advocated the violent overthrow of the U.S. government. All were convicted.

Following the Dunne case, the FBI expanded its SWP surveillance by utilizing a number of field offices nationwide. Although there were no significant criminal prosecutions against the SWP after 1942, the bureau's national security investigation of the party continued in operation until the official beginning of the SWP COINTELPRO in 1961.

The SWP COINTELPRO, which was the second COINTELPRO to be created by the bureau, was authorized by a Hoover memo dated October 12, 1961. This memorandum noted, in particular, that the SWP had been "openly espousing its line on a local and national basis through running candidates for public office and strongly directing and so supporting such causes as Castro's Cuba and integration problems arising in the South." It discussed other aspects of the new program and then said in conclusion, "Each office is, therefore, requested to carefully evaluate such a program and submit their views to the Bureau regarding initiating a SWP disruption program on a limited basis."[1]

A headquarters follow-up letter dated October 17, 1961, was sent to five selected field offices saying that "a disruption program along similar lines [to that against CPUSA] could be initiated against the SWP on a very selective basis."[2]

There can be little doubt that Hoover's decision to initiate this new COINTELPRO was shaped, in large measure, by the steady flow of documents that crossed his desk informing him of the ostensibly successful CPUSA COINTELPRO operation.

In selecting the SWP as a COINTELPRO target, Hoover had chosen a tiny political organization indeed: there were no more than 2,500 members nationwide.[3] Nevertheless—despite more than twenty years of surveillance of both the CPUSA and the SWP—Hoover, by 1961, had become alarmed over the prospect of a possible alliance between the two parties. This was an extraordinarily curious line of reasoning, in light of the historic enmity between the communists (Stalinists) and the socialists (Trotskyites). However, the director's logic was not to be questioned. This new COINTELPRO was to be known, within the bureau, as the "SWP Disruption Program."

The new program was to be administered, with Hoover's approval, by the SWP unit chief. Years later, this individual was asked why the FBI targeted the SWP in the first place. After all, the question went, the SWP was essentially hostile to CPUSA and thus useful in disrupting the communists. The FBI man pondered the question for a moment and then said, "I do not think that the bureau discriminates against subversive organizations."[4]

The bureau utilized its basic assortment of counterintelligence tools against the SWP with considerable skill. These methods—tested over the previous twenty years—included the use of undercover informants, electronic surveillance, disruption, and surreptitious entries (i.e., "black bag jobs").

The use of informants was extensive; about 85 percent of all SWP COINTELPRO operations utilized informants to gather information and create disruption. In this context, the word "informant" refers to non-bureau individuals (i.e., persons other than the special agents) who provided information to the FBI. Generally, information was supplied on a regular basis, for pay. Informants received direct supervision from FBI case agents attached to particular field offices. They generally reported two different types of SWP information to the case agents: "(1) what occurred at every meeting and every other activity he [the informant] attended, and (2) the name, address, physical description, place of employment and a great deal of other personal information about the SWP and YSA [Young Socialist Alliance] members, and their families."[5]

The SWP COINTELPRO lasted for ten years and utilized more than 1,000 undercover informants. The bureau paid out a total of $300,000 for their services. More than fifty informants held significant committee or executive positions within the party itself and they supplied more than 7,000 internal SWP document photocopies to the bureau.[6]

Some undercover informants' names are now known. Edward Heisler was a member of the Chicago branch of the Socialist Workers party. Heisler had his own set of keys to the SWP office, and had little difficulty in providing a steady supply of SWP documents to the Chicago field office from 1966 to 1971.

Ralph DeSimone was a secretary at the YSA branch in Berkeley, California. DeSimone had direct access to storage cabinets that held SWP minutes and documents. He would remove documents at night, have them photocopied, and return them before the YSA office opened the next day.

Electronic surveillance against the SWP included the use of telephone wiretaps and microphonic listening devices installed in meeting rooms, private offices, and homes. During the period from 1943 (when SWP surveillance actually began) until 1963, the FBI had wiretaps in place for a total of 20,000 wiretap days,and listening devices ("bugs") for about 12,000 days.[7]

The bureau made extensive use of black bag jobs. The term "black bag" refers to the black valises, generally filled with burglary tools, that were carried by special agents during surreptitious entry operations. In some situations these entries were for the purpose of installing listening devices. However, the overwhelming majority of surreptitious entries were for photographing or, in some cases, removing sensitive SWP documents and materials.

The materials photographed by special agents included contribution lists, membership lists, general correspondence, member photographs, transcripts of academic debates, union membership lists, policy statements, and travel schedules.

In time, the bureau developed its surreptitious entry of SWP offices into a fine art.

George Baxtrum, special agent-in-charge of the New York field office from 1953 to 1966 has explained how the black bag jobs usually worked.

Generally, a request for an entry had to be made by a special agent-in-charge to the appropriate assistant director in Washington. A surreptitious entry could not proceed without full approval in Washington and by the special agent-in-charge.

In the case of a new target, there would be a trial run. Then, often as soon as the next night, three special agents equipped with walkie-talkies but without weapons or identification would break into the target office. One would do the photographing and the other two would search for documents.

Virtually everything—desks, files, shelves, cabinets—would be searched. Several more special agents would be posted outside as lookouts. Usually a "slugger" was part of the lookout team. His job was to intercept anyone who might discover the operation in progress.[8]

Retired special agent M. Wesley Swearingen was involved in a number of black bag jobs. He remembers that "such risky assignments were illegal and that the special agents who carried them out were on their own in the event that they were discovered and arrested by local policemen." Swearingen has also observed that the agent-burglars tended to be unhappy men who were prone to ulcers and other tension-induced disabilities.[9]

Between 1958 and 1965 the SWP national office at 116 University Place in New York was the subject of eighty-one FBI break-ins. The SWP New York local office was entered seventy-six times. Three Young Socialist Alliance offices were entered sixteen times. Nearly 10,000 documents were removed or photographed during a total of more than 173 surreptitious entries.[10]

The COINTELPRO action against Morris J. Starsky for asserting his First Amendment rights was probably the most damaging of all the anti-SWP activities conducted by the FBI.

Starsky was an associate professor of philosophy at Arizona State University in Tempe, and he was also a member of the Socialist Workers party. He joined the ASU faculty in 1964 and quickly became involved in a number of liberal causes, including antiwar teach-ins on the campus. He supported virtually all SWP causes. In fact, he allowed his philosophy students to miss classes so that they could attend an antiwar rally at the University of Arizona in Tucson. Starsky later admitted that he was "a very controversial figure" at the university.

In the summer of 1968 Starsky and his wife were both named to be presidential electors by the Socialist Workers party. They also served the party as treasurer and as secretary.

The Phoenix FBI field office did not fail to notice Dr. Starsky's activities, and it identified him as an ideal COINTELPRO target. A May 31, 1968, COINTELPRO communication from Phoenix to headquarters outlined Starsky's activities in some detail and then stated that Starsky was "one of the most logical targets for potential counterintelligence action." Headquarters agreed.[11]

In the summer of 1968 the FBI made contact with the Arizona State University Board of Regents in an attempt to have the radical professor removed from the university payroll. The attempt was unsuccessful.

Next, the FBI monitored the professor's daily activities and found out that Starsky had been in a heated dispute with a young party worker over SWP funds and supplies. Other controversial incidents soon followed. The bureau then took a bold step. With Hoover's approval, the Phoenix field office mailed anonymous letters to all five members of the faculty Committee on Academic Freedom and Tenure. The letter contained a blistering attack on Starsky and his activities. It was strongly recommended that he be removed from the university altogether. The letter was signed "A Concerned ASU Alum."[12]

The faculty committee recommended that Starsky should not be removed from the faculty. By this time, however, the university board of regents saw the matter quite differently. In its opinion, Starsky had created far too much controversy. The board of regents arranged for the instructor—even though he was fully tenured—to take a one-year sabbatical from which he would not return to the university. The final Starsky memo to FBI headquarters noted that his reputation in the academic community was severely tarnished.

Thus, the COINTELPRO objective was achieved—an SWP professor had been removed from his teaching position. From the bureau's vantage point, the end result was entirely favorable.

Dr. Starsky's firing in June 1970 occurred just after the shooting at Kent State.

The damage inflicted on Starsky's academic career was permanent. "Morris knew he was on a blacklist," Mrs. Starsky now recalls. "Over the years he made hundreds of applications. But he never was able to get another decent job in teaching."[13] The fact that the FBI played a part in the Starsky dismissal was not fully realized until years later, when the fourteen pages of COINTELPRO documents were made available to Starsky under the Freedom of Information Act.

And only then did a federal court ultimately decide that the professor had been fired illegally; he was awarded $15,000. Also, as a result of the Starsky dismissal, the American Association of University Professors censured Arizona State for almost a decade.

Thus, the FBI's victory over the SWP was temporary in this instance. Everyone seems to have lost in the end.

In 1964 Frederick Rodney Holt was a mathematician with the Hickock Electrical Instrument Company in Cleveland, as well as chairman of the Ohio Committee for DeBerry and Shaw. Clifton DeBerry and Ed Shaw were the Socialist Workers party candidates for president and vice-president of the United States.

Mrs. Holt was a substitute music teacher for Fullerton Mound and

Union elementary schools in Cleveland. Her employer was the Cleveland Board of Education.

A confidential informant advised the FBI of the Holts' membership in the Socialist Workers party. The Cleveland field office, following up on this information, discovered that Mrs. Holt's position with the Cleveland school system was probationary.

The bureau went into action.

In a March 30, 1965, memo to FBI headquarters, the Cleveland field office requested the authority to contact the local board of education because "the SWP and YSA are a form of communist organizations and since communist oriented teachers are in such a critical position of influence." The bureau wanted Mrs. Holt out of the local public school system as soon as possible.[14]

Headquarters pondered the matter for a considerable length of time. A COINTELPRO memo dated August 6, 1965, authorized the Cleveland office—on a strictly confidential basis—to advise the school board of Mrs. Holt's affiliation with the SWP and YSA.[15] Special agents then contacted the school board in an effort to "preclude her from receiving a permanent appointment as a teacher."[16]

This COINTELPRO was ultimately successful. In a memo dated August 18, 1965, the Cleveland field office advised that "the Cleveland School Board will not renew the contract of Mrs. Holt for the coming year."[17]

More COINTELPRO documents concern the black political candidate Clifton DeBerry than any other member of the Socialist Workers party. DeBerry, a native of Holly Springs, Mississippi, grew up in the Chicago area and joined the Socialist Workers party in the early 1950s. DeBerry had previously been a union organizer for the Communist Party U.S.A. It was during his years with CPUSA that DeBerry earned the almost constant attention of the Chicago police. However, in time, political and philosophical differences developed between him and CPUSA, and he joined the Socialist Workers party.

Through no apparent fault of his own, DeBerry had a great deal of trouble holding onto a job during this time. Years later, after he had learned that the FBI was the source of most of his difficulties, he recalled, "I would get a job and it would last only 3 days. I would go from one job to another. The FBI would visit my boss and I would be fired."[18]

In addition to being an active SWP member, DeBerry was also involved in the civil rights movement. He became close friends with Malcolm X and other civil rights leaders.

In 1960 DeBerry moved to New York, and in 1963 he ran on the SWP ticket for councilman-at-large from Brooklyn, New York. He lost this local election, but did receive 3,514 votes. The party was pleased with the total.

On October 17, 1963, the special agent-in-charge of the New York field office sent a memo to the director in which he referred to DeBerry and noted that agents were attempting "to determine if there is anything derogatory in his background which might cause embarrassment to the SWP if publicly exposed."[19] An opportunity presented itself very quickly. Later in 1963, after DeBerry's election defeat in New York, the FBI learned that he was embarking on a nationwide speaking tour to raise funds for the party. This tour would include Chicago, where he would make a major speech before the Militant Labor Forum, and attend engagements at Northwestern University, Roosevelt University, and Navy Pier. The bureau also learned, through an undercover informant, that DeBerry had failed to keep up with his $30-per-week child support payments to his wife Hilda, then living in Chicago.

In an effort to cause as much embarrassment to the SWP as humanly possible, the bureau found a way to interrupt temporarily DeBerry's Chicago speaking plans for December 6, 1963.

The FBI contacted the Cook County Department of Welfare and advised officials there that Clifton DeBerry—the same Clifton DeBerry who was behind on child support payments to his wife in Chicago—was in town. The Welfare Department wasted no time in obtaining a warrant, and DeBerry was arrested on charges of nonsupport. The arrest occurred right in the meeting hall just before DeBerry was to begin his speech—a sensational embarrassment!

DeBerry was taken to the Chicago Municipal Court, where he posted bond. Somewhat distracted by all of this, he nevertheless returned to give his speech to the Militant Labor Forum.

On December 10, 1963, DeBerry was found guilty of nonsupport and sentenced to six months in the Chicago House of Corrections. His sentence was changed to probation when DeBerry agreed to stay current with his child support payments.

The results of this disruptive COINTELPRO action were confirmed by memo to the director on December 19, 1963. The communication closed by saying that "after a reasonable time Chicago will ascertain disposition of this case through established sources."[20]

Following this episode Clifton DeBerry was nominated, on January 7, 1964, to be the Socialist Workers party candidate for president of the United States. The DeBerry–Shaw ticket ran unsuccessfully on a strong anti–Vietnam War platform. And in 1965 DeBerry ran, without success, for mayor of New York.

During 1964–65, in an attempt to undermine these two Clifton DeBerry campaigns, the FBI produced and mailed anonymous and derogatory letters and news releases to its friendly media contacts. In many cases, these media contacts were reporters and editorial personnel with whom the bureau had worked for years. Curiously, however, this effort fell flat. A number of COINTELPRO documents refer to the fact that the media simply did not publish the DeBerry stories. The files provide no explanation.

One researcher has since interviewed DeBerry about his thoughts during those years. He asked if DeBerry knew that there was an official COINTELPRO action against him. In answering, DeBerry recalled a conversation he had in Chicago with a police officer whom he had known for some time. The officer took him aside and said, in a quiet voice, "somebody who is high up is really interested in you."[21]

Evelyn R. Sell, a native of Cleveland, attended a high school in Detroit and received a B.A. in elementary education from Wayne State University in 1965. She had joined the Socialist Workers party in 1948, was active in party affairs, and ran unsuccessfully in 1968 on the party ticket for the Michigan State Board of Education. From 1965 to 1969 Sell was a teacher at the Burton Elementary School in Detroit. During this time she earned the reputation of being an intelligent and exceptionally well qualified teacher.

Mrs. Sell moved to Austin, Texas, in 1969. In Austin, she was employed by the Austin Independent School District in the Head Start program for preschool children. Sell also helped to found a branch of the Socialist Workers party in Austin.

The FBI had known of Sell's SWP membership for some time. The bureau learned of her move to Texas through an undercover informant. At this point, she became an official COINTELPRO target.

The San Antonio field office asked the Austin Police Department to make contact with Ernest Cabe, the assistant superintendent of schools in Austin. The bureau wanted the local police officials to provide Cabe with information and documents regarding Sell's Socialist Workers party background.

The contact was made by the Austin police in late 1969. After considering what the police had told him about Sell, Assistant Superintendent Cabe decided to take no action at that time.

In March 1970, however, FBI special agents contacted Cabe directly. The COINTELPRO document regarding this meeting, dated March 31, 1970, noted that "the decision not to issue a new contract or consider the subject [Sell] is based on information received from [deleted] of the Austin police department."[22]

M. K. Hage, Jr., then the president of the Austin School Board, remembers that "the social climate was such that we would fire anyone who was a socialist."[23]

It was at about this time that Evelyn Sell realized the FBI was investigating her. "My cards were up on the table," she recalls. "It was the FBI and the Austin School District officials who were underhanded."[24]

Sell was soon able to find a new job within the Human Opportunities Corporation (HOC), which also had a Head Start program. The FBI continued to apply pressure. Three of Sell's supervisors were contacted by special agents. The bureau's message was essentially the same: Evelyn Sell is a socialist. She does not deserve to have a job!

Sell was advised by her employer of the new FBI contact. HOC officials were outraged by the FBI efforts. They seriously considered filing a harassment lawsuit against the bureau.

Neither Sell nor HOC gave in to the FBI. Evelyn Sell left HOC on her own accord in 1972.

Maude White Wilkerson, a black elementary-school teacher working in Washington, D.C., unknowingly became a COINTELPRO target in 1969. She was employed by Head Start at the time and was highly regarded by her colleagues.

Wilkerson had joined the Young Socialist Alliance while a student at the American University. The FBI, again working through an undercover informant, learned of her political affiliation.

A COINTELPRO memorandum concerning Wilkerson came from FBI headquarters to the Washington field office on April 11, 1969. It instructed the local special agent-in-charge to "consider available steps that can be taken of a counterintelligence nature to have the subject separated from her employment as a teacher."

The memo also noted that Wilkerson's (her name was then Maude White) father was a Methodist minister and would undoubtedly be in "opposition to the tenents [sic] of YSA."[25]

On April 23 the Washington field office reported—again on the basis of information supplied by an informant—that the subject's mother was visiting the subject's apartment while a local YSA meeting was in progress. Thus, an anonymous letter to her parents was ruled out.

The April 23 memo also pointed out that Wilkerson was not married but had been living with a man named Terrill Brumback, a YSA organizer. In addition, another YSA member named Joe Miles was also spending nights at her apartment.[26]

On May 7, 1969, headquarters instructed the Washington field office to prepare an anonymous and derogatory letter about Wilkerson. This letter, ostensibly from a neighbor of Wilkerson's, was to be sent to the superintendent of the Washington, D.C., school system.[27] It was typed on plain bond typewriter paper and mailed in a plain white envelope to Superintendent William C. Manning on June 3, 1969.

The letter was scorching. It began by asserting that Wilkerson "has been holding weekly meetings of a Socialist Youth group." The meetings, the letter said, were held on Sunday nights and were attended by about twenty individuals.

The third paragraph dropped the bombshell: "This group advocates an overthrow of our present form of government in a way similar to the Cuban revolution of Fidel Castro." In this same paragraph, the "anonymous neighbor" states, "I bring this information to your attention in order to protect the D.C. school system from the menace of a teacher who does not have the interests of the children or country at heart." The letter was signed "A Concerned Citizen."[28]

The bureau was unable to determine Dr. Manning's immediate reaction to the letter. However, another COINTELPRO document—dated July 3, 1969—indicates that the Intelligence Unit at the Metropolitan Police Department had also made inquiries concerning Wilkerson's association with alleged subversive organizations.[29]

Wilkerson had earned an excellent teaching reputation and had no intention of retiring. As she recalls, "Being a teacher, especially in the D.C. schools, I saw how rotten the schools were, how much money was spent on the war and how little on education."[30] Fortunately, Dr. Manning saw no good reason why the young teacher should leave her position. Wilkerson also received support from the National Education Association. John Radcliff, then head of Wilkerson's chapter, recalls that "as soon as I found out about the situation I called the school district and told them that . . . we, acting as the union, would absolutely and categorically not tolerate anyone messing with Maude's job."[31]

The matter ultimately came to nothing. Since the Head Start program was not totally funded by the federal government, the FBI decided not to consider a national security case against Maude Wilkerson.

In 1967 Walter R. Elliott—then age thirty-four and married—was the scoutmaster of Boy Scout Troop 339, which met every week at Park Avenue School in Orange, New Jersey. Elliott was employed by a Chevrolet dealership in Newark, lived in Orange, and devoted a considerable amount of his spare time to scouting activities. Elliott was married to an active member of the Socialist Workers party.

Although not a party member himself, Elliott had attended a number of party-membership meetings, some of which were held in his own home.

At a meeting held in the Elliott home in November 1967, an undercover FBI informant allegedly heard Joe Carroll, an organizer of the Newark branch of the SWP, tell Elliott that he "should quit fooling around with the scouts and join the Socialist Workers party." Elliott is reported to have replied that "he thought he could better influence young minds by staying where he is."[32]

This conversation was immediately reported to the FBI. At this point, the bureau looked into the matter in depth.

It was verified through contact with the Boy Scouts' national headquarters in Brunswick, New Jersey, that Elliott was indeed an active scoutmaster. The Newark field office determined, however, that its files contained "no public source of information of a subversive nature concerning Elliott."[33]

It was also verified that Elliott's wife was the subject of an ongoing FBI security investigation because of her Socialist Workers party membership. Officials at FBI headquarters evidently saw this situation as a possible opportunity for the SWP to infiltrate part of the scouting organization.

Thus, on November 15, 1968, a COINTELPRO authorization was sent to the Newark field office. It was captioned "Walter Radcliff Elliott—SWP Disruption Program."[34]

The Newark field office was instructed to contact the Boy Scouts' national headquarters again, to advise them that Elliott had a subversive background. The memo cautioned (as it almost always did) against embarrassing the bureau or revealing confidential sources.

The derogatory information about Elliott was given to the Boy Scouts' national headquarters on January 19, 1968. The bureau learned, after making follow-up calls, that the Orange Mountain Council of the Boy Scouts would not approve Troop 339's application for charter renewal as long as it was led by Elliott. These results were confirmed by a COINTELPRO memo dated July 29, 1968. The bureau also noted that Elliott's removal "from the Scouting program, where he would have strong influence in shaping of the minds of young boys, reflects the successful application of the disruption program for a worthy cause."[35]

Obviously, the principle of guilt by association must apply to this situation. The bureau had launched a successful SWP disruption program against an individual who was not, in fact, an SWP member at all.

Thus, the SWP COINTELPRO—although comparatively small—included targets in many parts of the country. In most cases, the targets themselves were caught completely off guard.

For example, two non-SWP-member students at Oberlin College participated in an antiwar hunger strike that was evidently sponsored by the YSA. The FBI sent anonymous letters to the parents of these students warning of "damage to their son's academic standing."

The letter also said that "left wing students" were "cynically using the boy." A follow-up letter stated to the parents "that you may not be aware of John's current involvement in left wing activities."[36]

In San Antonio, Texas, the bureau was successful in getting an SWP-member teacher fired from her job even though she was widely regarded "as an excellent teacher."[37]

The Denver field office sent an anonymous letter to the Denver School Board from "a concerned mother," detailing the SWP affiliation of board candidate Allen Taplen.[38]

In the fall of 1969, the New York field office sent an anonymous and disruptive letter to the black New York SWP mayoral candidate Paul Boutelle. Boutelle was known to have a quick temper, and he had been quite outspoken about possible racism within the ranks of the SWP. The bureau, in an attempt to aggravate the situation as much as possible, mailed the letter to Boutelle at his home in the Bronx. The letter suggested that Boutelle should "hook up with the Panthers where you'd feel at home. Maybe then we could get on with the job Trotsky had in mind for us." Signed, "Your nasty friends."[39]

On September 19, 1969, the *New York Times* reported that the SWP candidate's name was being removed from the mayoral ballot because the Board of Elections ruled that most of the signatures on the SWP petition were invalid.[40]

The FBI had earlier attempted to discredit John Clarence Franklin, the Socialist Workers party candidate for Manhattan borough president in 1961. In this situation, the bureau provided Franklin's criminal record to a columnist for the *New York Daily News*. The criminal background information was published in detail.[41]

In other actions, the FBI—under the guise of concerned parents—sent anonymous letters to the top officials of a number of major universities including Indiana University, the University of Texas, and the American University. These letters expressed outrage that the Young Socialists Alliance had been recognized as a legitimate campus organization at their universities.

In 1965, special agents of the Detroit field office prepared an anonymous and wholly fictitious letter that was sent to the Michigan Democratic State Central Committee and six additional Democratic party organizations. Bureau officials had suggested to the special agents that this letter "should be prepared on a manual typewriter using commercially purchased stationery. If possible, you should consider the use of stationery containing the title or seal of the Wayne State University." The final draft appeared to have been written by a student at the university. It alleged that the campus Democratic club had been infiltrated by the Young Socialists Alliance. It also named the leader of the YSA and warned that the Socialist Workers party was on the attorney general's list of subversive organizations.[42]

The San Francisco field office sent a highly disruptive letter to Sam Jordan, the black independent candidate for mayor. This letter, mailed in 1963, urged the candidate to completely disassociate himself from his SWP campaign workers.[43]

Sally L. Moore lost her job as a distribution clerk with the U.S. Post Office in 1969. The Civil Service Commission had determined that, because of her SWP membership, she was unsuitable for employment.[44]

In 1969 Kenneth Evenhuls applied for a position as an air traffic controller with the Federal Aviation Administration. The FBI supplied information regarding Evenhuls's SWP membership to the Civil Service Commission. He was denied FAA employment.[45]

An FBI headquarters memo dated April 21, 1971—soon after the Media office burglary—seems to have finally brought COINTELPRO operations against the Socialist Workers party to a halt.[46]

As with the CPUSA COINTELPRO, the SWP COINTELPRO had extracted an enormous cost in human misery. Careers were destroyed, jobs were lost, friendships and affiliations were ended, and reputations were tarnished. First and Fourth Amendment rights had been arbitrarily brushed aside.

The total scope of the bureau operations against the SWP all but defies any rational justification. Consider the more than 173 surreptitious entries and the removing or photographing of 10,000 private SWP documents, the use of more than 1,000 SWP undercover informants at a cost of more than $300,000, the deployment of 36,000 wiretap and listening-device days. All of this enormous effort was initiated against an organization that had less than 2,500 members in 1961.[47]

Interestingly, over the course of the entire COINTELPRO operation, the FBI found absolutely nothing of a criminal nature. Indeed, there was no indication that any undercover FBI informant "ever observed any violation of federal law or gave information leading to a single arrest for any federal law violation."[48]

What, then, was the reason for this wasteful assault on such a tiny group? The impetus, of course, came from Hoover himself. At the time that the SWP COINTELPRO began in 1961, Hoover had been director for thirty-seven years. He had become both obsessive and—in the case of the Trotskyite SWP—myopic.

NOTES

1. FBI Memorandum, J. Edgar Hoover to Special Agent-in-charge, New York Field Office, 12 Oct. 1961.

2. FBI Memorandum, J. Edgar Hoover to Special Agents-in-charge, 17 Oct. 1961.

3. "A Fight for Political Rights," Political Rights Defense Fund, New York, 1986, pp. 18–19.

4. Senate Select Committee to Study Governmental Operations with Respect to Intelligence Activities, "Supplementary Detailed State Reports on Intelligence Activities and the Rights of Americans," Book III, 94th Cong., 2d sess., 14 Apr. 1976, p. 18.

5. "A Fight for Political Rights," Political Rights Defense Fund, p. 18.

6. "A Fight for Political Rights," Political Rights Defense Fund, pp. 17–20.

7. Margaret Jayko, ed., *FBI on Trial* (New York: Pathfinder, 1988), p. 50.

8. Senate Select Committee to Study Governmental Operations with Respect to Intelligence Activities, "Warrantless Surreptitious Entries: FBI 'Black Bag' and Microphone Installation," Book III, 94th Cong., 2d sess., 14 Apr. 1976, pp. 355–65.

9. John M. Crewdson, "Details on FBI's Illegal Break-ins Given to Justice Department," *New York Times*, 27 Jan. 1969, p. 9.

10. Jayko, *FBI on Trial*, p. 73.

11. FBI Memorandum, Phoenix Field Office to Headquarters, 31 May 1968.

12. Nicholas M. Horrock, "Files of FBI Showed It Harassed Teacher," *New York Times*, 29 Jan. 1975, p. 12.

13. Tom Fitzpatrick, "Morris Starsky's Proud Exit," *Valley News and Arts Journal*, 17 Feb. 1989, p. 2.

14. FBI Memorandum, Cleveland Field Office to Headquarters, 30 Mar. 1965.

15. FBI Memorandum, Headquarters to Cleveland Field Office, 6 Aug. 1965.

16. FBI Memorandum, Washington, D.C., Field Office to Cleveland Field Office, 6 June 1965.

17. FBI Memorandum, Cleveland Field Office to Headquarters, 18 Aug. 1965.

18. Nelson Blackstock, *COINTELPRO: The FBI's Secret War on Political Freedom* (New York: Pathfinder, 1988), pp. 69, 78.

19. FBI Memorandum, New York Field Office to FBI Headquarters, 17 Oct. 1963.

20. FBI Memorandum, Chicago Field Office to FBI Headquarters, 19 Dec. 1963.

21. Blackstock, *COINTELPRO: The FBI's Secret War*, p. 80.

22. FBI Memorandum, San Antonio Field Office to FBI Headquarters, 31 Mar. 1970.

23. Blackstock, *COINTELPRO: The FBI's Secret War*, p. 162.

24. Ibid.

25. FBI Memorandum, FBI Headquarters to Washington, D.C., Field Office, 11 Apr. 1969.

26. FBI Memorandum, Washington, D.C., Field Office to FBI Headquarters, 23 Apr. 1969.

27. FBI Memorandum, FBI Headquarters to Washington, D.C., Field Office, 7 May 1969.

28. FBI Memorandum, Washington, D.C., Field Office to FBI Headquarters, 23 May 1969.

29. FBI Memorandum, Washington, D.C., Field Office to FBI Headquarters, 3 July 1969.

30. Blackstock, *COINTELPRO: The FBI's Secret War*, p. 166.

31. Ibid., p. 167.

32. FBI Memorandum, New York Field Office to FBI Headquarters, 29 Nov. 1967.

33. Nicholas M. Horrock, "FBI Harassed a Leftist Party," *New York Times*, 19 Mar. 1975, p. 1.

34. FBI Memorandum, Headquarters to Newark Field Office, 15 Nov. 1968.

35. FBI Memorandum, Newark Field Office to FBI Headquarters, 29 July 1968.

36. Eugene Kaza, telephone interview with author, 23 Oct. 1989; FBI Memorandum, FBI Headquarters to Cleveland Field Office, 29 Nov. 1968.

37. Blackstock, *COINTELPRO: The FBI's Secret War*, p. 161.

38. Ibid., pp. 41–42.

39. FBI Memorandum, FBI Headquarters to New York Field Office, 8 Oct. 1969.

40. "Another Party Ruled Off the Ballot," *New York Times*, 19 Sept. 1969, p. 39.

41. Cathy Perkus and Noam Chomsky, *COINTELPRO: The FBI's Secret War on Political Freedom* (New York: Monad Press, 1975), p. 91.

42. John M. Crewdson, "FBI Checking of Radicals Went On beyond Deadline," *New York Times*, 6 Oct. 1975, p. 1.

43. FBI Memorandum, FBI Headquarters to San Francisco Field Office, 21 Oct. 1963.

44. Jayko, *FBI on Trial*, p. 79.

45. Ibid., p. 80.

46. FBI Memorandum, FBI Headquarters to Field Offices, 21 Apr. 1971.

47. "Fight for Political Rights," Political Rights Defense Fund, pp. 20–26.

48. Jayko, *FBI on Trial*, p. 50.

4 The White Hate Group COINTELPRO

Edgar, I want you to put people after the Klan and study it from one county to the next.

Lyndon B. Johnson

The night of June 12, 1964, was hot and muggy. A blue 1963 Ford station wagon, registered to the Congress of Racial Equality and bearing Mississippi license plate H25503, was racing at more than 100 miles an hour down Mississippi Highway 19—a two-lane stretch of paved road between Philadelphia and Meridian.

The occupants of the station wagon almost certainly knew that their lives were in danger. The driver, a black civil rights worker named James Chaney, was a native of Meridian. Michael Henry Schwerner, one of the passengers, was a white social worker from New York and a graduate of Cornell University. The other passenger—also a white New Yorker—was Andrew Goodman, a student at Queens College.

All three were members of COFO, the Council of Federated Organizations, and were part of the huge influx of civil rights workers into Mississippi in the summer of 1964. The COFO was organized to increase black voter registration, establish freedom schools, and develop black community centers in Mississippi. The COFO presence, comprised of more than 600 mostly out-of-state workers, was bitterly resented by most whites in Mississippi.

Two cars were pursuing the speeding station wagon: a Neshoba County sheriff's patrol car driven by Deputy Sheriff Cecil Price, and a Ford driven by a man named Doyle Barnette. Each car had three passengers. All were members of the White Knights of the Ku Klux Klan.

At some point in the chase, Deputy Price turned on the patrol car's red flasher light. James Chaney must have felt that he could not outrun the deputy. Chaney pulled off on a side road and stopped at a wooded spot near the town of House, Mississippi. It was a fatal miscalculation.

Price brought the patrol car to a stop behind the station wagon. He left the red flasher light on. Barnette, driving the other car, came to a halt behind Price.

Deputy Price, a large round-faced man weighing over 200 pounds, walked up to the station wagon, looked at Chaney, and said, "I thought you were going back to Meridian!"

"We were going," Chaney replied.

"You sure were taking the long way around. Get out of the car," Price said.[1]

Price opened the station wagon's front door and violently pulled Chaney from behind the wheel. Then Goodman and Schwerner were ordered from the car. They were pushed into the backseat of the patrol car. Chaney, who had been standing next to the wagon, started to follow his companions into the patrol car. Suddenly—without warning—Price, using his blackjack, hit Chaney with a savage blow to the head and threw him bodily into the backseat with the other two.

A Klansman named Jimmy Arledge got behind the wheel of the station wagon, and the three cars made a slow procession on the gravel road to a point about halfway between Meridian and Philadelphia. The terror that must have occupied the minds of the three civil rights advocates at this point can scarcely be imagined. The vehicles stopped.

Schwerner, Goodman, and Chaney were then ordered from the patrol car. They were surrounded by the Klansmen. All was silent. Then suddenly, one Klansman—probably Wayne Roberts—grabbed hold of Michael Schwerner and spun him around so that the two were face to face.

"Are you a nigger lover?" Roberts demanded.

"Sir, I know just how you feel," Schwerner replied.[2]

Roberts was holding a .38 caliber revolver in his right hand. With his left hand on Schwerner's shoulder, he pointed the barrel at the civil rights worker's chest and pulled the trigger. In the country dark, flame could be seen at the end of the barrel. The .38 slug hit Schwerner's left lung and he fell to the ground. Death was surely instantaneous.

There was no chance whatever for the other two to escape. Goodman was grabbed and held. There was another shot. The .38 slug hit Goodman in the lung and penetrated to the thoracic area. He fell to the ground.

Klansman Jim Jordan called, "Save one for me!"[3] He approached Chaney, who was already suffering from a head wound. The black man was slowly backing up near the road. Jordan shot Chaney three times—in the head, the back, and the stomach.

The bodies of the young men were loaded into the back of their own station wagon. They were taken to Old Jolly Farm, a spread owned by Olen Burrage. They were buried in a shallow grave at a site where a cattle pond was being constructed. Within a few days almost fifteen feet of dirt was piled on top of them. The Ford station wagon was burned near the Bogue Chitto Swamp.

The news that the three civil rights workers were missing captured the attention of the nation. The apparent kidnapping was very much in keeping with the dramatic spread of Klan terror during the first half of 1964.

Attorney General Robert F. Kennedy wanted immediate federal action. In a memo to President Johnson he noted that, in large measure, the spread of Klan terror had the actual sanction of local law enforcement agencies in many parts of the South. The attorney general, the president, and virtually the entire Johnson administration felt that the spread of Klan terror in general—and the apparent kidnapping in Mississippi in particular—was an intolerable situation.

Those within the FBI who knew of the CPUSA COINTELPRO felt that the bureau should move, and move quickly, against the KKK in the same manner it was then moving against the Communist Party U.S.A.

On July 2, Johnson told Hoover, "Edgar, I want you to put people after the Klan and study it from one county to the next. I want the FBI to have the best intelligence system possible to check on the activities of these people."[4]

In recalling the summer of 1964, Ramsey Clark (who was himself to become attorney general under Lyndon Johnson in 1967) remembers, "Mr. Johnson showed that he could do more with Mr. Hoover than anybody who had ever tried."[5]

Hoover did indeed move. The new investigation, code-named "Miburn" (Mississippi Burning), was promptly set in motion. A new FBI office was built in Jackson, Mississippi.

As the FBI was moving into action, Klan violence in the South and black violence in the North escalated. During July, August, and September of 1964, twenty-seven Southern black churches were burned to the ground. Concurrently, black riots swept major cities in Pennsylvania, New York, New Jersey, and Illinois.

At almost the same time, more than 500 FBI special agents together with Justice Department lawyers and investigators, plus a contingent of U.S. Navy personnel to assist in the search, were brought into the Mississippi investigation. The three dead civil rights workers were found on August 4.

The investigation and trial were pursued with a relentless intensity until seven very hard-core Klansmen were sent to prison five years and nine months later. On December 29, 1967, Federal Judge Harold Cox sentenced Imperial Wizard Sam Bowers and Wayne Roberts each to ten years in prison. Deputy Cecil Price and Billy Wayne Posey received six-year prison terms. Jimmy Arledge, Jimmy Snowden, and Doyle Barnette were sentenced to three years in prison. The eighth Klansman, Jim Jordan, had already been given a four-year sentence.

At the time that the Jackson field office was established, in July 1964, the FBI internal supervision of Klan activities was transferred from the General Investigation Division to the bureau's Domestic Intelligence Division. It would be supervised by William C. Sullivan. In effect, the Klan investigation was moved from the criminal to the intelligence division.

On July 30 Hoover asked for a study to determine if a sustained counterintelligence program directed at white hate groups, located primarily in the South, should be initiated. Less than a month later, on August 27, the Intelligence Division recommended the immediate initiation of a "hard hitting closely supervised coordinated counterintelligence program to expose, disrupt, and otherwise neutralize the Ku Klux Klan and specified other hate groups."[6] At that time the total KKK membership stood at 14,000 members.

On September 2, 1964, a headquarters memorandum was sent to seventeen selected FBI field offices. This memo created the White Hate COINTELPRO. The field offices were to target seventeen Klan organizations as well as the American Nazi party, the National States Rights party, and other such groups.[7]

The FBI had a difficult assignment in hostile territory.

In the states of the Old South there were no black U.S. marshals, no black circuit court judges, no black U.S. commissioners, no black district court judges, and no black jury commissioners. Thus, a black involved in a federal court action in the South would go all the way through the judicial process without seeing one black official.[8] In addition, the FBI special agents knew that they could not count on the wholehearted support of local law enforcement officials.

With these facts in mind, the seventeen FBI field offices were instructed to open active control files and then, after consideration, assign White Hate COINTELPRO files to special agents who were familiar with racist organizations. The field offices were instructed to submit to headquarters their anticipated counterintelligence actions against White Hate targets in their respective territories on or before October 15, 1964.

The techniques to be utilized in this COINTELPRO were similar to those used against the Communist Party U.S.A. and the Socialist Workers party. The White Hate targets were the first COINTELPRO targets that had no connection in any way with a foreign intelligence movement or international revolutionary organization. As one bureau official said in 1964, these were "homegrown tomatoes."[9]

Virtually the entire arsenal of techniques was brought to bear against white hate organizations with a level of success that can only be described as extraordinary.

During the almost seven years of the White Hate Group COINTELPRO, the bureau received 404 proposals from the field offices for specific counterintelligence actions against primarily Klan targets. Out of these proposals, 289 actions were actually implemented, with known results achieved from 139 actions.[10]

One very popular technique involved sending anonymous or fictitious materials to Klan members. While specific results were sometimes difficult to document, FBI undercover informants operating within the Klan reported a dramatic impact on Klan morale. These mailings were used to spread rumors, create distrust and dissension, and generally disrupt and neutralize Klan activities.

One of the most effective of the direct mail tools was—of all things—a simple postcard.

Postcards were sent anonymously and often featured derogatory cartoons of KKK members. The messages were simple and powerful. One card read, "Klansman, trying to hide behind your sheets? You received this and someone knows who you are!"[11] The postcards played on the Klan's traditional secrecy—its greatest strength.

Another card said, "Which Klan leaders are you spending your money on?"[12] This card was designed to suggest that Klan leaders were using rank-and-file membership dues to finance high living.

Another card—again hitting at the Klansman's sense of secure anonymity—said, "Klansman, someone is peeking under your sheet."[13]

The bureau's mailing lists came primarily from Klan membership information that had been stolen by informants or from license plates that had been photographed or observed at Klan rallies. Some cards were sent to the Klansman's residence deliberately to cause disruption within his family. In other situations, cards were sent to the Klansman's place of work. If the postcards did not get the subject fired, they did sometimes cause mistrust or apprehension among employers or employees.

In keeping with normal COINTELPRO practices, the bureau moved very carefully. Any possible exposure of counterintelligence procedures was meticulously anticipated. As was the customary procedure with other COINTELPROs, only a limited number of personnel in each field office knew anything at all about the programs. The addressing of cards and/or anonymous letters was done either by hand or on older, and generally out-of-use, typewriters. When addressing by hand, penmanship styles were altered slightly. Only typewriters not used for regular bureau correspondence could be brought into service for these special projects. Cards and letters were mailed outside of field office cities. Mailings were spread over a period of several days, and only a few would be mailed at a time. The post office was not to get the impression that a mass mailing was being conducted. Addresses were limited to individuals who had been positively identified as Klan members. Anonymous letters and envelopes were produced on commercially purchased nonwatermarked paper.

The Cincinnati field office sent its first group of postcards to local Klan members in April 1966, and the response was immediate.

The May 24 editions of the *Cincinnati Inquirer*, the *Columbus Citizen Journal*, and the *Dayton Daily News* all featured stories with the headline, " *'YOU ARE KNOWN MEMBERS OF THE KLAN,' OHIO CARDS SAY.*"[14]

One Cincinnati-area Klansman said that the cards "were very embarrassing." He added that "someone has apparently gotten hold of our membership rolls. Some post office employees and neighbors of these people (KKK members) are getting some juicy items for gossip."[15]

William C. Duff, then U.S. postmaster in New Concord, Ohio, remembers that the pink postcards were first seen in a mailbox along U.S. 40. "We thought," he recalls, "that someone passing through town dropped them off."[16]

A spokesman for the Cincinnati FBI office issued the statement that "we don't know who is behind it."[17]

The Cincinnati office was achieving its COINTELPRO objective: disruptive and exposure of Klan members in Ohio. Additional mailings were to follow.

In another part of the country, an undercover informant advised bureau intelligence officials on June 27, 1966, that members at the Georgia-based Klavern 41 of the United Klans of America (UKA) were extremely disturbed by an FBI postcard mailing in their area.[18] One member, speaking with great emotion at a June 24, 1966, klavern meeting, said that whoever was responsible for such a mailing might well be the type of individual who would shoot Klansmen in the dark![19]

The Crawfordville, Georgia, klavern was hit hard by the mailings. Indeed, the citizens of Crawfordville—after learning about the cards—voiced their strong opposition to the Klan at local church, political, and civic meetings. At one Klan meeting shortly after a postcard mailing, only five people attended from the Crawfordville area.

The Richmond, Virginia, field office also made effective use of the postcards. Two hundred were mailed to Klan members throughout the area in June 1966.[20] According to informants working within the local klaverns, a number of Klan members said they had received cards, and expressed concern that their privacy had been penetrated by someone they did not know. The Richmond office reported that attendance at Klan functions had dropped substantially. The postcard mailings were kept up for two years.

The bureau continued to employ new and sometimes novel ways to neutralize white hate organizations. One ideas was to draw members away from the Klan and into a completely fictitious organization. Within the bureau, such an organization was referred to as "notional." An organization with the almost comically ironic name of "The National Committee for Domestic Tranquility" (NCDT) was dreamed up by the bureau's Counterintelligence Unit, a division of the Internal Security

Section. Eventually, the "National Committee" had chapters—at least on paper—in nineteen states. This nonexistent committee was headed by "Harmon Blennerhasset"—a nonexistent person.[21]

A newsletter was mailed from "Blennerhasset's" address of P.O. Box 124, Dayton, Ohio 55412.

Generally the FBI targeted klaverns where tension was known to exist already or where it was deemed possible to recruit new informants. Members who could be pinpointed as being involved in factional disputes were perfect targets.

The newsletter was prepared by the bureau's Exhibit Section on a specially designed "National Committee" letterhead, and it was sent directly to targeted Klan members on a regular basis.

One of the first newsletters, outlined in a COINTELPRO memorandum dated May 4, 1966, was directed at abasing the grand dragon of the United Klans of America, Knights of the Ku Klux Klan, State of Virginia.[22]

At times it is hard to believe that the FBI White Hate targets were grown men. The bureau was able to hit Klan members repeatedly with strategies that often seem quite obvious, however cunningly they were devised. For example, a special card enclosed with the Virginia newsletter boldfaced a parody of the basic Klan membership card, which features the lettering "AKIA" for "A Klansman I Am." The FBI enclosure featured the lettering "AKIW" and then held, within the basic design, the letters "ACIA"—meaning "A Klansman I Was, A Christian I Am."[23]

The memo noted that "the anonymous distribution of the attached letter and enclosure may appeal to those Klansmen who are deeply mystic."[24] It is true that historically the Klan has attempted to identify itself with conservative American patriotism, politics, and religion. Nevertheless, it is all but impossible to imagine a truly mystic Klansman. By the same token, it is equally difficult to imagine that someone within the FBI actually believed such a Klansman existed.

The following excerpt from the May 4 memo was, in any case, a typical "National Committee" letter; its appeal featured a mixture of old-time religion and right-wing politics. There was a concerted effort to make the Klansman insecure with his own klavern.

My fellow Americans,

The recent response to the National Committee for Domestic Tranquility evidenced by the mass exodus of Klansmen from the United Klans of America in the great State of Virginia has revitalized our belief that present day Klan leaders are, in general, in league with the Anti-Christ.

The belief that the Anti-Christ seeks to destroy the Christian world was recently demonstrated by the Grand Dragon of the United Klans of America in Virginia, when he publicly attacked, insulted, and damned the Baptist Church which had introduced him to Christ. The public rejection of Christ by a leading Klan official demands sincere meditation and reflection.

The Eternal Book of Life shall bear the inscription of the faithful who stood in the face of adversity and publicly pronounced their commitment to Christ.

That we, the created, step back from the passing scene to make certain that our lives are directed towards eternal heavenly acceptance, is an urgent demand.

The Good Book, in the Sermon on the Mount, and in other inspired passages, not only brings us the word of heavenly life for the deserving, but also, thricefold, warns us of the eternal damnation of the living hell.

Knowing full well that the conduct of our personal affairs will warrant us an eternal life, be it Heaven or be in Hell [sic], is it not fitting that we, the faithful, urgently offer a commitment to Christ so as to avoid the damnable fire of Hell that will separate the falling soul from the Almighty, and the blessed departed kinfolk for an eternity of years?

The decision is simple, the result—the simplicity of eternal beauty or the complexity of despair. If your choice brings the despair, you shall not ask, "Oh Lord, why have you forsaken me?" as you will then see, with blistering assurance, that it is you who have forsaken Him.

We, former Klansmen all, who bear witness in the light of day, urgently beseech you to embrace our public commitment to Christ, and disavow the path of the Anti-Christ, delivered to you, the misdirected souls, on the sugary, forked tongues of deceitful Klan leaders.

For you who seek Christ and reject the Klan, we have enclosed a membership card announcing your commitment to Christ.

To join with us, merely display this card in your home which will demonstrate to those who are really concerned about you that "A Klansman I Was, A Christian I Am."

> Harmon Blennerhasset
> Executive Director
> National Committee for
> Domestic Tranquility
> Dateline Dayton[25]

Letters like this had a very strong impact. On May 24, 1966, an undercover informant within Lawrence Lodge 610, of the UKA in Montgomery, Alabama, reported great concern at the most recent meeting. Members wanted to know what on earth was going on. Who was sending these newsletters? How did they get the names? Wasn't the KKK a secret? What else do they know? If there are informants, they must be found! No other Klan business was discussed.

Four months and three newsletters later, some Klansmen had had enough. Membership began to drop. The ultimate White Hate COINTELPRO objective—to neutralize the Klan—was being achieved.[26]

Other strategies were also at work. The New Orleans field office used the classic snitch-jacket technique against the UKA in Louisiana and created the impression that the local assistant grand dragon was a police informant when, in fact, he was not. A communication written on "National Committee" letterhead was sent to the assistant dragon. It addressed him as an informant and thanked him for his cooperation. The letter was sent by the bureau with the full knowledge that the grand dragon read every single piece of mail that came to the Klan post office box in New Orleans.

The grand dragon went into a "furious tantrum" and demanded that the assistant dragon be removed from any Klan business until the matter was settled.[27]

An extremely acrimonious Klan meeting was held on September 5, 1966, in West Monroe, Louisiana. The falsely accused assistant dragon demanded that the actual evidence regarding him be produced. Insults and shouting followed, and the matter deadlocked. A Klan trial was planned for October.

As far as the FBI was concerned, the damage had been done. In a COINTELPRO memo dated September 21, 1966, the New Orleans office advised that the harm to Klan morale had been considerable, regardless of the outcome of the pending trial. Disruption and suspicion had been planted within the ranks. Soon—as was generally the case—the attendance of younger members began to drop. The klavern was, in effect, neutralized.[28]

The Birmingham, Alabama, field office stated in a COINTELPRO memo dated January 5, 1967, that Birmingham-area Klan members were shaken by the arrival of the anonymous NCDT newsletters within their klavern: "There has been almost no trouble or disturbance by the UKA or any other hate group in the Birmingham division during the last three months." The memo added that such Klan inactivity could be attributed, in large measure, to "the counterintelligence activity by the bureau."[29] While the writer of this memo was undoubtedly engaging in hyperbole to some degree, the record does in fact show that Klan activity came to a virtual standstill at this time.

In November 1966 the Jackson, Mississippi, *Clarion Ledger* ran an article based partly on information supplied by the bureau. This article—not entirely true—said that the Mississippi Klan was being abolished altogether and that the imperial wizard was quite unable to control the situation.

In January 1967 an edition of the "National Committee for Domestic Tranquility" newsletter was mailed to provide Klan penetration for all seventeen FBI field office areas of responsibility. The newsletter, again blending old-time religion and grassroots right-wing politics, took dead aim at Imperial Wizard Robert Shelton. The selected paragraphs below give an idea of its style.

On grassroots conservatism:

That you fully understand the position of the NCDT is our only objective. We hold that it is most necessary for all Americans to fully support our national effort in Vietnam. We believe that this great effort requires the understanding and moral support of each and every God-fearing American. That our brave men cannot long endure without our wholehearted support and prayers is a self-evident truth.

On Robert Shelton:

The Imperial Wizard whom you have so blindly followed, spews a special kind of venom which has reduced the Klan to a totalitarian organization which well serves the interests of the communists. If you still listen to him without evaluating his words, you also may be duped into diverting the public interest from the great problems at hand which must be tended to.

On encouraging distrust:

Shelton will not provoke us as he has provoked others. Your committee is growing in strength and Klan leaders who place God and country before Shelton and Shekels are among us.

On encouraging disruption:

Those of you who have not talked with anyone from the NCDT
as yet, be strong of heart; you may join with us in spirit by firmly
resolving to attend no more the meetings of the UKA.

On encouraging the Klansman to distrust his organization:

I have never met a klansman who did not love his country, but I
have met those of Shelton's men who are strictly professional
money men and organizers; those who have no real interest in our
Southland. It is they whom you must divorce yourselves from.

Best wishes for a Happy New Year

> Harmon Blennerhasset
> Executive Director
> National Committee for
> Domestic Tranquility
> Dateline Dayton[30]

As previously noted, FBI COINTELPRO operations were handled with
great secrecy. Information regarding the programs was distributed only
on a need-to-know basis. Hoover knew that if COINTELPRO information was compromised or fell into the wrong hands the program would
be in jeopardy.

In one action in 1967, the bureau was almost exposed. An NCDT
newsletter was sent to a number of top Klan officials in North Carolina.
In effect, it "fired" the North Carolina grand dragon for misconduct and
incompetence in office and also took Imperial Wizard Robert Shelton to
task for not firing the North Carolina official himself. Just how this other
(fictitious) organization could dismiss an official within the KKK was
never explained. In any event, the FBI had hit an exposed nerve. Shelton
was irate. He complained, without knowing who sent the letter, to both
the FBI and the U.S. Post Office. He asserted that someone was guilty
of mail fraud. The bureau told Shelton that the matter was out of its
jurisdiction. Nevertheless, bureau officials in the Intelligence Division
and the director himself became nervous. Special agents contacted the
Chief Postal Inspections Office and asked what action it planned to take
in the Shelton matter. The FBI was told that the matter had been referred
to the Criminal Division of the Justice Department. To their relief, FBI
officials learned that there would be no investigation. Justice Department
lawyers, in explaining their decision, told Special Agent C. D. Brennan

that Shelton's complaint appeared "to involve an internal struggle for control of Ku Klux Klan activities in North Carolina and since the evidence of mail fraud was somewhat tenuous in nature the post office did not contemplate an investigation."[31]

At no time did anyone in the FBI inform any other government office that the bureau itself was the culprit.

Another racist organization—the National States Rights party (NSRP)—planned to hold its national convention at the Holiday Inn on Stocking Street in Jacksonville, Florida, on June 6 and 7, 1969. This information was given to the bureau by an NSRP informant. Action was taken very quickly.

After approval from headquarters, an anonymous letter dated June 5, 1969, was sent directly to the Holiday Inn manager. It was mailed—as usual—in a plain envelope. The letter itself was typed on plain non-watermarked stationery and signed "A Concerned White Citizen."[32]

The letter pointed out that Holiday Inn, "the nation's innkeeper," was not being very selective in taking in guests. The National States Rights party—as the letter stated—opposed any form of integration, and believed and acted on the belief that blacks and Jews were responsible for most, if not all, of the problems in the United States. The "concerned citizen" also said he was thinking about sending a copy of the letter to the local sheriff and other officials; he was worried that black hoodlums would descend on the Holiday Inn and Jacksonville to disrupt the convention.

On June 6 the manager contacted the Jacksonville FBI office and the local sheriff. He also contacted the Holiday Inn regional office in Atlanta, which decided that, after this convention, no other NSRP conventions would be held at a Holiday Inn!

Thus, a certain amount of disruption had been accomplished by the FBI action. To the considerable dismay of those attending the convention, police were very visible at the Holiday Inn. Also, and perhaps of even more concern, was the obvious fact that the NSRP had an informant within their membership.[33]

The FBI Miami office used the anonymous mailing technique with effectiveness against the assistant grand dragon at Klavern 4 of the United Klans of America, in the Miami area. Using stolen Klavern 4 member lists, the bureau sent mailing cards that featured a cartoon and photograph showing the assistant grand dragon to be a personal friend of Fidel Castro![34]

The klavern was forced to conduct an investigation of their own grand dragon—who was, of course, not a friend of Fidel Castro. The mailing also created animosity between Klavern 4 and state Klan officials. Indeed, as the weeks went by, the suspicions and name-calling grew so great that the target himself resigned from his post.

There was even further damage. The state KKK organization, alarmed over the prospect of a communist within Klavern 4, revoked the klavern's charter. Following this, infuriated Klavern 4 members resigned from the KKK altogether.

Thus, one letter, a complete fabrication, had encouraged many Klansmen to resign and put a klavern completely out of business. The special agents who had engineered this action were warmly congratulated by the director and Domestic Intelligence Division officials in Washington.

The practice of writing and sending anonymous letters could become quite ruthless and nasty. The letter below was sent to the wife of Robert Shelton and to the wives of three other Klan leaders.

My Dear Mrs. _____

I write this letter to you only after a long period of praying to God. I must cleanse my soul of these thoughts. I certainly do not want to create problems inside a family but I owe a duty to the klans and its principles as well as to my own menfolk who have cast their divine lot with the klans.

Your husband came to   about a year ago and my menfolk blindly followed his leadership, believing him to be the saviour of this country. They never believed the stories that he stole money from the klans in   or that he is now making over $25,000 a year. They never believed the stories that your house in   has a new refrigerator, washer, dryer and yet one year ago was threadbare. They refuse to believe that your husband now owns three cars and a truck, including the new white car. But I believe all these things and I can forgive them for a man wants to do for his family in the best way he can.

I don't have any of these things and I don't grudge you any of them neither. But your husband has been committing the greatest of the sins of our Lord for many years. He has taken the flesh of another unto himself.

Yes, Mrs. , he has been committing adultery. My menfolk say they don't believe this but I think they do. I feel like crying. I saw her with my own eyes. They call her Ruby. Her last name is something like and she lives in the 700 block of Street in . I know this. I saw her strut around at a rally with her lust-filled eyes and smart-aleck figure.

I cannot stand for this. I will not let my husband and two brothers stand side by side with your husband and this woman in the glorious robes of the klan. I am typing this because I am going to send copies to Mr. Shelton and some of the klans leaders that I have faith in. I will not stop until your husband is driven from and back into the flesh-pots from wherein he came.

I am a loyal klanswoman and a good churchgoer. I feel this problem affects the future of our great country. I hope I do not cause you harm by this and if you believe in the Good Book as I do, you may soon receive your husband back into the fold. I pray for you and your beautiful little children and only wish I could tell you who I am. I will soon, but I am afraid my own men would be harmed if I do.

A God-fearing klanswoman[35]

As we have seen, confidential informants supplied almost all of the necessary inside information for the bureau's disruptive mailings directed at the KKK. Historically, the bureau has tended to classify its informants into two basic categories: subversive, and extremist. Subversive informants are generally used to investigate groups or individuals who are known to have or are believed to have the intention of "overthrowing, destroying or undermining the Government of the United States." Extremist informants, on the other hand, are used to infiltrate organizations that may ve subversive to some degree and also violence prone, but whose primary aim is to "deny the rights of individuals under the Constitution."[36] The KKK and similar organizations fit into the latter category.

Former Klan informants now recall that they reported on everything imaginable concerning the klaverns and individual KKK members. In addition, they took or usurped everything they could get their hands on including personnel records, membership lists, and financial information.

By the end of 1965, about a year and a half after the White Hate

COINTELPRO officially began, the bureau had more than 2,000 under-cover informants in place and operating within the klaverns. This meant that about 15 percent of the entire KKK was comprised of informants. About half were elected to leadership positions.

William C. Sullivan, head of the Domestic Intelligence Division during the years of the rapid expansion of the White Hate COINTELPRO, re-membered later that "the decision was made (in 1956) to incorporate all counterintelligence operations into one program directed against the Communist Party. I merely redirected the use of those techniques toward investigating the Klan."

"We made it known to the Klan," Sullivan said, "that their own prejudices and ignorance had made them patsies for their own people." Sullivan said that the bureau "created suspicion throughout the whole damn Klan, which was their undoing."[37]

Klan units in Lincoln County, Mississippi, were heavily infiltrated by informants in 1964. As a result of this infiltration, the Jackson field office was furnished with a complete local membership list.

After studying the information in detail, special agents privately in-terviewed every single Klan member on the list. The results were note-worthy. In a memo dated January 28, 1965, the Jackson field office reported that, as a result of the FBI interviews, the Lincoln County Klan had burned all of its records.[38]

One Mississippi unit, normally comprised of more than 100 members, quickly dropped to sixteen. Within a short period of time after the in-filtration and interviews, only five units in Mississippi were operating at full strength. By January 1965, 40 percent of the Mississippi mem-bership had stopped paying regular dues and 30 percent had withdrawn from the KKK.

The Klan organizations in North Carolina were also heavily infiltrated. In the North Carolina situation, the bureau discovered that there were tensions within the organization, and issued press releases that an-nounced an impending split. A number of North Carolina newspapers ran the story.

The rift did indeed occur. Much, if not all, of the credit belongs to the skillful use of informants. In September 1967, 150 dissident North Car-olina Klansmen demonstrated their dissatisfaction with the leadership. They nailed their cards to a cross and set the structure on fire. The bureau advised news photographers of the event, and it received front-page coverage throughout the state.

J. Edgar Hoover had this type of KKK disruption program in mind when—in a letter addressed to Attorney General Ramsey Clark—he said, "We have found that by the removal of top Klan officers and provoking scandal in the state Klan organizations, the Klan in a particular area can be rendered ineffective."[39]

In one of the more innovative techniques used against the Klan, informants set up a notional organization that was an entirely fictional Klan. Its membership was made up of unsuspecting members. This notional Klan became the UKA's rival. Its purpose was to attract members away from the United Klans of America—thus making the two KKKs compete for membership at both the state and local level. In 1967 the rival, notional Klan had a roster of 250 members. It was directed by the FBI.

Sometimes unusual opportunities for disruption were discovered by informants. In the fall of 1965, for example, an informant discovered that a long-term member of the Knights of the Ku Klux Klan (a separate organization from the UKA) had been receiving a veteran's pension based on a 100-percent disability. However, this same Klansman was also self-employed in a small contracting business with earnings of about $400 per month. The local field office contacted the Veterans Administration with this information. The Klansman's monthly checks stopped immediately.

The matter did not end there. The FBI also contacted the Internal Revenue Service. The IRS, as might be imagined, took a very dim view of the fact that this individual had not paid taxes on his two incomes for a period of years. Had the bureau's informant not infiltrated the Klan, it is quite likely that the situation would never have been discovered. As it was, another Klansman had been effectively neutralized.

In North Carolina, informants discovered an illegal kickback operation that was being conducted by members of the United Klans of America. One Klan member was selling insurance to other members of the North Carolina Klan and depositing a portion of the premiums with the local Klan treasury. The operation was quite successful and supplied revenue to the KKK for many years. Special agents took immediate action and advised the insurance company that their firm's premiums were helping to finance the KKK in North Carolina. The firm canceled all policies.

In some situations the bureau stepped into the judicial process. In Miami in 1965, a Klan leader who had been convicted on a weapons charge was out on bail pending his appeal. The Klansman would have been well advised to stay home until his appeal was to be heard. He didn't. He spoke at a local Klan rally. Miami special agents arranged to have news photographers present. The resulting newspaper articles, together with photographs, were given to the appellate judge who was scheduled to consider the case.

The undercover work in the White Hate COINTELPRO was largely a stunning success; but undercover informants often did not receive precise instructions from their FBI handlers, and sometimes informants engaged in activities that were clearly illegal. One informant who worked inside the KKK for five years remembers that he and Klan members had "beaten people severely, had boarded buses and kicked people off; went in restaurants and beaten them with blackjacks, chains, pistols."[40] He also described taking part in Klan attacks on Freedom Riders at the Birmingham, Alabama, bus depot, where "baseball bats, clubs, chains and pistols were used in beatings."[41]

In most cases, informants were told in advance that there was considerable risk they may be involved to some degree in violent activity. One agent later described the position an informant was often put into: "It is kind of difficult to tell him that we would like you to be there on deck, observing, to be able to give us information and still keep yourself detached and uninvolved and clean, and that was the problem we constantly had."[42]

Often informants could not stop the Klan from committing acts of extreme violence without blowing their cover. This was particularly true when informants had penetrated the activist cells within the individual klaverns.

One informant explained that the basic Klan informant duties were "to go to meetings, write up reports . . . on what happened, who was there, . . . to try to totally identify the background of every person that was there, what their relationships were, who they were living with, who they were sleeping with, to try to get some sense of the local structure and the local relationships among the people in the organizations."[43]

An FBI special agent who worked with Klan informants said that the Ku Klux Klan informants "furnished us information on the meetings and the thoughts and feelings, intentions and ambitions, as best he knew them, of other members of the Klan, both in the rank and file and the leadership."[44]

The FBI informant penetration of the KKK was every bit as thorough as it had been in the Communist party program. In 1964 J. Edgar Hoover—exaggerating somewhat—said, "We have been able to penetrate the Klan. There are 480 Klansmen in Mississippi. I had our agents in Mississippi interview every member of the Klan there just to let those individuals know the FBI knew who they were and had an eye on them."[45]

But the undercover operations often put the government in the very compromising position of participating in violence in order to monitor it.

The story of Gary Thomas Rowe, Jr., is a good illustration of this.

Rowe was an FBI informant within the Birmingham, Alabama, Klan for five years and took his bureau work very seriously. Rowe joined the KKK in 1961 and worked as a bartender in the VFW club in Birmingham. As a Klan informant, Rowe's basic duties consisted of attending meetings, determining where members lived, determining members' marital status and also their political affiliations. This type of assignment is called "missionary work." He was urged to spread rumors, and was cautioned against involvement in violence.

After the murder of the three civil rights workers near Philadelphia, Mississippi, Rowe was told that "the Man (Hoover) has declared war on the Ku Klux Klan and that, anything you can do and you're man enough to do, do it."[46] He was paid $400 a month plus expenses.

Rowe was told of the code word "COINTELPRO" by Special Agent MacFall of the FBI Birmingham office. MacFall told Rowe never to use the word in conversation. Further, if Rowe did hear the word he was to drop everything he was doing and contact the FBI immediately. In the context relevant to Rowe and his FBI handler, the use of the word "COINTELPRO" meant that a new counterintelligence initiative was being started against the Klan or that changes were being made in an existing operation.

Rowe was able to pull all membership data from the Klan files, as well as obtaining confidential files from the Birmingham Police Department. Everything was given to the bureau for photocopying. Gary Rowe was on hand for Klan national meetings and conventions, and he turned all meeting data over to the FBI immediately after the events had ended.

Rowe now recalls, "I don't know at any given two weeks of my career for over five years that there was not some Klan activity, day or night."[47] Sometimes he contacted the FBI as often as five times a day. Rowe had listening devices in his car. His instructions were to spend as much time as possible in his car. He was instructed to get his Klan passengers to talk about Klan activities.

On the night of March 25, 1965, Gary Rowe's career as an undercover informant changed forever. He was thirty-one at the time.

On the afternoon of March 25, about 12,000 civil rights demonstrators gathered for a massive rally in front of the state capitol at Montgomery, Alabama. Mrs. Viola Liuzzo, a white mother of five from Detroit, was there as a civil rights volunteer. As a volunteer it was her job to help transport demonstrators from Montgomery to Selma.

At 7:34 P.M. she was making a return trip toward Montgomery. She was driving a 1963 Oldsmobile with Michigan license plate EJ9177. Sitting beside Liuzzo in the front seat was a nineteen-year-old black youth named Leroy Moton.

Earlier that day Rowe, accompanied by Klansmen Collie Leroy Wilkins, Jr., Eugene Thomas, and William Orville Eaton, had gone to Montgomery to watch the rally. Their primary mission was to monitor the civil rights activities and, if possible, cause disruption.

The four men were riding in a 1962 red-and-white Chevrolet Impala. Rowe was sitting in the backseat. As they were driving through Selma they noticed an out-of-state car that was being driven by a white female and had a black passenger. They decided to follow Liuzzo's car as it headed toward Montgomery.

The Klansmen followed the Liuzzo car on Highway 80. Eugene Thomas said, "We're going all the way on this one. We came to get a black and white together!"[48]

The Chevrolet slowed through a radar checkpoint and then, at about the spot where Highway 80 narrows to a two-lane highway, accelerated to more than 100 miles an hour to catch the fast-moving Liuzzo car. The Klansmen pulled out into the passing lane next to the Liuzzo car.

It was 8:13 P.M.. As the two cars were traveling side by side at more than 80 miles an hour, the Klansmen rolled down their windows and fired into the Liuzzo car. A .38 bullet hit Viola Liuzzo. Her head and hands jerked violently and her mouth opened as if to scream. The bullet entered the left side of her head close to the junction of her jawbone. It passed through her spinal cord at the base of her brain and lodged there. She died instantly. The car was hit several times. Somehow Leroy Moton kept the car under control until it stopped. He survived.

Rowe maintained that he did not fire. Nonetheless, there had been an FBI undercover informant in the car with the murderers. Rowe became the government's star witness against the three Klansmen who were convicted.[49]

In spite of, or perhaps because of, the Liuzzo killing and the Philadelphia murders, the FBI—again pressured by President Johnson—continued to pursue the Klan with a vengeance until the end of the White Hate Group COINTELPRO in the spring of 1971.

The KKK was, for all practical purposes, decimated by the end of 1968.

Undercover informants were used in 85 percent of the Klan actions. At one point, the FBI had so thoroughly infiltrated the Klan that Hoover briefly considered installing an informant at the top of the Klan, and thus making Klan policy.

By 1971 the KKK membership had declined from a high of 14,000 members in 1964 down to 4,300 members.

To be sure, the murderous fury of the KKK had been contained by the FBI, but was it done at the expense of the Constitution? In containing and neutralizing the KKK, the FBI did some damage to constitutional liberties. This is one of those situations that test the fundamental basis of American liberty. Indeed, how much liberty should be given to those who would destroy it?

These words written more than 100 years ago by the English constitutional jurist Sir Thomas May ask much the same question: "Men may be without restraints in their liberty; they may pass to and fro at pleasure; but if their steps are tracked by spies and informers, their words noted down for crimination, their associates watched as conspirators—who shall say that they are free?"[50]

NOTES

1. Don Whitehead, *Attack on Terror: The FBI against the Ku Klux Klan in Mississippi* (New York: Funk & Wagnalls, 1970), p. 181.

2. Ibid., p. 183.

3. Ibid.

4. Ibid., p. 91.

5. Richard Gid Powers, *Secrecy and Power* (New York: Macmillan, 1986), p. 408.

6. FBI Memorandum, Intelligence Division to the Director, 27 Aug. 1964.

7. FBI Memorandum, FBI Headquarters to the Atlanta Field Office, 2 Sept. 1964.

8. Victor S. Navasky, *Kennedy Justice* (New York: Atheneum, 1977).

9. Senate Select Committee to Study Governmental Operations with Respect to Intelligence Activities, "Charles D. Brennan Testimony, 13 June 1973," Book III, 94th Cong., 2d sess., 14 Apr. 1976, p. 10.

10. House Committee on the Judiciary, Civil Rights and Constitutional

Rights Subcommittee, *Hearings on FBI Counterintelligence Programs*, 93rd Cong., 2d sess., 20 Nov. 1974, Serial No. 55.

11. FBI Memorandum, Cincinnati Field Office to FBI Headquarters, 5 Apr. 1966.

12. Ibid.

13. Ibid.

14. " 'You Are Known Members of Klan,' Ohio Cards Say." *Cincinnati Inquirer*, 24 May 1966.

15. Ibid.

16. Ibid.

17. Ibid.

18. FBI Memorandum, Savannah Field Office to FBI Headquarters, 27 June 1966.

19. Ibid.

20. FBI Memorandum, Richmond Field Office to FBI Headquarters, 1 July 1966.

21. Frank J. Donner, *The Age of Surveillance* (New York: Alfred A. Knopf, 1980), p. 210.

22. FBI Memorandum, FBI Headquarters to Field Offices, 4 May 1966.

23. Ibid.

24. Ibid.

25. Ibid.

26. FBI Memorandum, Headquarters to Field Offices, 21 Sept. 1966.

27. Ibid.

28. Ibid.

29. FBI Memorandum, FBI Birmingham Field Office to Headquarters, 5 Jan. 1967.

30. FBI Memorandum, Headquarters to Field Offices, 24 Jan. 1967.

31. Senate Select Committee, "Charles D. Brennan Testimony," Book III, pp. 64–65.

32. FBI Memorandum, Jacksonville Field Office to Headquarters, 26 June 1969.

33. Ibid.

34. FBI Memorandum, F. J. Baumgardner to W. C. Sullivan, 18 Apr. 1966; FBI Memorandum, Headquarters to Miami Field Office, 28 Apr. 1966.

35. FBI Memorandum, Richmond Field Office to Headquarters, 26 June 1966.

36. Senate Select Committee to Study Government Operations with Respect to Intelligence Activities, "Use of Informants in FBI Domestic Intelligence Investigations," Book III, 94th Cong., 2nd sess., 14 Apr. 1976, pp. 233–34.

37. William C. Sullivan with Bill Brown, *The Bureau: My Thirty Years in Hoover's FBI* (New York: W. W. Norton, 1979), pp. 130–31.

38. FBI Memorandum, Jackson Field Office to Headquarters, 28 Jan. 1965.

39. FBI Memorandum, Director to the Attorney General, 19 Dec. 1967.

40. Senate Select Committee, "Use of Informants in FBI Domestic Intelligence Investigations," Book III, see Deposition of Gary Thomas Rowe, Jr., 17 Oct. 1975, at p. 12.

41. Testimony of Gary Thomas Rowe, Jr., before Senate Select Committee, 2 Dec. 1975.

42. Ibid.

43. Ibid.

44. Senate Select Committee, "Use of Informants in FBI Domestic Intelligence Investigations," Book III, see Special Agent No. 3, 21 Nov. 1975, at p. 242.

45. Sanford J. Unger, *FBI: An Uncensored Look behind the Walls* (Boston: Little, Brown, 1975), p. 415.

46. Senate Select Committee, "Use of Informants in FBI Domestic Intelligence Investigations," Book III, p. 12.

47. Ibid., p. 24.

48. FBI Birmingham, Alabama, Field Office, File H 44–1236, 26 Mar. 1965.

49. Senate Select Committee, "Use of Informants in FBI Domestic Intelligence Investigations," Book III, p. 12.

50. Thomas May, *Constitutional History of England* (1863), p. 275, cited in Senate Select Committee, "Use of Informants in FBI Domestic Intelligence Investigations," Book III, p. 227.

5 The Black Nationalist Hate Group COINTELPRO

We knew it wasn't going to be a tea party but we didn't
anticipate how violent the U.S. government would get.

Ron Karenga
United Slaves

The incident began routinely enough.

On the oppressively hot night of August 11, 1965, Los Angeles mo-
torcycle patrolman Lew W. Minikus briefly pursued and then stopped
a twenty-one-year-old drunk driver named Marquette Frye. Frye was
black. It was about 7:00 P.M. when Minikus approached Frye's vehicle,
which had stopped at the corner of 116th and Avalon streets in the Watts
district of Los Angeles.

Frye, accompanied by his brother Ronald, was in no mood to be
arrested by a white policeman. Harsh words were exchanged as the
young black resisted arrest. Pushing and shoving followed. An angry
crowd began to gather as police reinforcements arrived. A few rocks
and bottles were thrown and there was a tense standoff. However, by
some miracle, the black crowd began to subside. By 1:00 A.M., a huge
Los Angeles police contingent had successfully controlled the situation.

The next day, however, the Watts district exploded in electrifying fury. A racial disorder of such magnitude had never before been seen in the United States. For three days, Watts convulsed with savage fire-fights and indiscriminate looting and destruction. Almost 16,000 law enforcement personnel, including police, sheriff's deputies, and National Guardsmen, moved in to restore order.

All told there were 4,000 arrests, 34 deaths, 1,300 injuries, and $35 million in property damage.[1] Although black riots had occurred in the United States before, Watts was the first race riot to capture national attention. It is no exaggeration to say that Watts was a turning point. After August 1965, race relations in the United States were never the same again. Watts, in fact, was the first in a series of race riots that traumatized the nation during the summers of 1965, 1966, 1967, and 1968.

Most of the riots were sparked by a minor incident, usually involving the police. Most escalated to involve looting, tear gas, and firefights, sometimes with automatic weapons. In total, the race riots of the 1960s accounted for at least 225 deaths and 4,000 injuries, and more than $100 billion in property damage.[2] The collective psychological damage was beyond measurement.

Lyndon B. Johnson, chief architect of the Great Society, was shattered. "By every traditional index of progress—of wages earned, of housing, of entry into high public service, of education, of integration in the armed forces—the black community was, in the 1960's, moving forward more rapidly than ever before in American history."[3] The president's anguish over black violence was profound. He wanted answers. He turned to the FBI for help.

Answers were not easy. Originally, the government suspected that communists or some other foreign influences might be involved. This was not the case.

As a general practice, the bureau had kept track of racial agitators by use of its Security Index, which, as we have seen, was developed during the Roosevelt administration. From the 1950s on, this listing was generally comprised of about 15,000 individuals who were regarded as dissidents. Although more than 1,500 blacks were usually named on the Security Index, none were felt to endanger the security of the nation.

Over the years (also as a general practice), bureau special agents had followed civil rights groups to determine, primarily, if these groups were under any form of foreign influence—communist or otherwise. Generally, there was no evidence of such influence.

In 1960 the FBI maintained microphonic surveillance on just "one black separatist group." By 1963 the microphonic surveillance had increased to "two black separatist groups" and "one black separatist functionary."[4] The findings from these projects were less than startling.

A good part of the surveillance of Dr. Martin Luther King, Jr., occurred within the Communist Party U.S.A. COINTELPRO. Here too, as noted in Chapter 2, there was very little evidence to suggest that black organizations or black leaders in the United States—in spite of the most inflammatory rhetoric—were part of a communist conspiracy at all.

In 1964, after the small-scale ghetto uprisings of that summer, the president instructed the FBI to investigate and determine the origins and extent of racial unrest. Director Hoover, almost certainly after conferring with the president, made the bureau's report public in September 1964. Nine cities has been studied. Information was gathered from "public officials, police officers, clergymen, leaders of responsible organizations and individuals considered to be reliable." There was no evidence of any kind to suggest "that the riots were organized on a nation-wide basis."[5]

In 1965, after the Watts riot, FBI field offices were instructed to be alert for and provide information regarding "planned racial activity such as demonstrations, rallies, marches."[6]

In late 1966 a number of FBI field offices were ordered to prepare monthly and in some cases semimonthly reports of "existing racial conditions in major urban areas." Special agents were instructed to utilize "established sources"[7] in ghetto areas. These reports were to be used by the FBI in Washington to analyze the activities of virtually all civil rights organizations, black nationalist hate groups, and any other hate groups known to function in ghetto areas.

Thus, by early 1967, the FBI was utilizing considerable resources to keep the White House, the Justice Department, the military, and the other intelligence agencies within the federal government up to date.

After riots in Newark and Detroit later in 1967, President Johnson announced that the FBI had standing instructions "to search for evidence of conspiracy." In addition, internal field-office directives instructed special agents "to conduct a continuing survey to develop advance information concerning racial developments with clearly point to the possibility of mob violence and riotous conditions." Surveillance targets included "black nationalist groups" and "hate-type organizations with a propensity for violence."[8]

That year, 1967, turned out to be the most violent year of all. With reference to the Detroit riots, Lyndon B. Johnson remembered that "the events of July 24–28, 1967, will remain forever etched in my memory. The phone rang at 3 A.M. on the morning of July 24. Attorney General Ramsey Clark was on the line."[9] From that point on, it was all downhill. The Detroit violence was unparalleled. Before it was over, federal troops had been sent in.

By September, racial violence had erupted in sixty-seven cities. Thirty-two people had been killed and 3,200 were injured. Property damage exceeded $100 million.[10]

In an address to the nation, Johnson said, "We will not endure violence." He gave a special warning to public officials nationwide: "If your response to these tragic events is only business as usual you invite not only disaster but dishonor."[11]

Against this backdrop of extreme violence, J. Edgar Hoover was developing the next COINTELPRO.

The president and Hoover had been close friends for many years, and the director was a regular visitor to the Oval Office. They agreed that a new counterintelligence program had to be developed—one that would, if possible, intercept and neutralize violent black activists. Such an effort, as a matter of course, would almost certainly improve and supplement other FBI programs, other Justice Department programs, and the intelligence efforts of the military.

The documents creating the new COINTELPRO were drafted during the third week of August 1967. An August 25 memorandum initiating the new COINTELPRO was sent via registered mail to twenty-three field offices strategically located in cities across the United States. The memo came directly from Hoover. All copies were sent directly to the special agents-in-charge.[12]

Field offices were instructed to "establish a control file" immediately and assign responsibility for following and coordinating this new counterintelligence program to all experienced and "imaginative" special agents "with experience in working with black nationalists, hate-type groups and organizations." Special agents were well equipped to fill this need.[13] By 1967 more than 1,000 agents were receiving intelligence on civil rights groups each month. The effort might have been more successful, though, if black agents had been used for many of these assignments. However, in 1967 black agents comprised only 2 percent of all special agents working for the FBI.

The purpose of the new COINTELPRO was to "expose, disrupt, misdirect, discredit or otherwise neutralize the activities of black nationalist hate type organizations."[14] The August 25 memo—more than two and a half pages of single-spaced instructions—specified that groups for special attention would include the Congress of Racial Equality, the Nation of Islam, the Student Non-violent Coordinating Committee, the Deacons of Defense and Justice, and the Southern Christian Leadership Conference.

Individual extremists targeted for special attention included Maxwell Stanford, H. "Rap" Brown, Stokely Carmichael, and Elijah Mohammed. The memo closed with the traditional warning that "under no circumstances should the existence of the program be made known outside the bureau."[15]

Including the Southern Christian Leadership Conference with the original group of COINTELPRO targets was an odd move. Section Chief George C. Moore recalled, "At that time it was still under investigation because of the communist infiltration. As far as I know, there were not any violent propensities, except that I note, in the cover memo [executing the Black Nationalists COINTELPRO] or somewhere, that they mentioned that if Martin Luther King decided to go a certain way, he could cause some trouble. . . . I cannot explain it satisfactorily."[16] The Black Panthers were not mentioned in the August 25 memo because they had not yet risen to national recognition.

Less than a month after the beginning of the new Black Nationalist Hate Group COINTELPRO, the Justice Department expanded and refined its administrative machinery for evaluation "of civil disturbance intelligence." The FBI was to be a vital part of this expansion.

In a memorandum dated September 14, 1967, Attorney General Ramsey Clark continued to broaden the FBI's basic intelligence authority. Clark advised the bureau that "sources or informants in black nationalists organizations, SNCC and other less-publicized groups"[17] should be developed and expanded to determine the size and purpose of these groups.

This "Ghetto Informant Program" was to function concurrently with the new COINTELPRO. It grew rapidly. By 1968 some 3,000 ghetto informants were being used; by 1969 the program had grown to 4,000 informants, and there were 7,000 by 1972.[18]

The program was designed to establish listening posts in the black areas of virtually every major city in the United States. Informants were recruited from many walks of ghetto life. In many cases, the informants were property or business owners. Some were the parents and grandparents of militants. Veterans and especially members of veterans' organizations proved to be excellent informants. All lived in or worked in ghetto areas, and all were paid regularly for their information.

The primary objective—as outlined in an October 1967 Justice Department memo—was to develop "additional penetrative coverage of militant black nationalist groups and the ghetto areas immediately to be in a position to have maximum intelligence in anticipation of another outburst of racial violence next summer."[19]

Informants attended and reported on open meetings of extremist groups and attempted to identify underground outlets for extremist literature and weapons. Every effort was made to determine racial feelings and attitudes—particularly, quick changes in attitudes. Foreigners in the ghetto were watched. The Justice Department was advised every two weeks on the possibility of riots and their most likely times and locations.

Additionally, Ramsey Clark created the Interdivisional Intelligence Unit in December 1967. The IDIU accepted and classified the large volume of incoming FBI reports. These data were categorized and filed within a vast Justice Department master index system designed for quick reference. In time, the IDIU was processing almost 3,000 reports a month.[20]

Even when the new programs were in place, the director and the top associates of the bureau were still nervous. The prospect of another riot-filled summer was almost too awful to contemplate. Hoover decided to expand the programs. On March 4, 1968, Hoover expanded the Black Hate COINTELPRO from twenty-three to forty-one offices. He also announced to the field offices the long-range goals for this COINTELPRO: the prevention of the unification of black nationalist groups and the possible rise of a "black Messiah," neutralization of potential trouble-makers, discreditation of the groups in the eyes of the black community as a whole, and the prevention of recruitment of youths.

Field offices were to advise headquarters of the local special agent assigned to coordinate this new COINTELPRO at the field office level.

In addition, field offices were instructed to provide immediately a summary of local black nationalist movements, listings of all black nationalist organizations, as well as suggestions for COINTELPRO actions. Reports, which were to be submitted every ninety days, were to use the following captions: operations under consideration, operations being effected, tangible results, and developments of counterintelligence interest.[21]

The director followed almost immediately with another memo, which stated, "The Negro youth and moderate must be made to understand that if they succumb to revolutionary teaching, they will be dead revolutionaries."[22]

Hoover's expansion more than doubled the size of the COINTELPRO by the late winter of 1968. In hindsight, it seems strange that what was to become the most feared of all the black nationalist organizations was not even mentioned in the August 1967 or March 1968 COINTELPRO directives.

The Black Panther party—originally known as the Black Panther Party for Self Defense—was founded in October 1966 by Huey Newton and Bobby Seale, both students at Merritt College in Oakland, California. Its purpose was to provide a unified black response to the perceived police brutality in the Oakland area. Actually, it went much further than that. Huey Newton remembered later that "the police, not only in the Oakland community, but throughout the black communities in the country were really the government."[23] And Bobby Seale recalled, "Basically we wanted land, bread, housing, education, clothing, justice, and peace."[24] Many blacks felt as if they were living in a colony that was ruled by white police.

Panther members began to appear in public openly carrying weapons and wearing black berets and leather jackets, but their first official action was a minor one: directing traffic. An intersection at the Santa Fe Elementary School in North Oakland was considered dangerous for children to cross. A traffic light had been needed for years. Two of the Panthers had gone to school there. The Panthers arrived, in full battle gear, to see that the children crossed safely. It wasn't long before the much-needed light was installed.

Panther members began patrolling the crime-infested slums of Oakland. They became active in protesting rent evictions of blacks and in counseling welfare recipients. They monitored the actions of the Oakland Police Department and worked with black prisoners. Others soon joined, including author and Panther Minister of Information Eldridge Cleaver, Kathleen Cleaver, David Hilliard, Donald Lee Cox, Emory Douglas, and others.

The organization stepped into the national spotlight when its members made a brazen entrance at the California State Legislature on May 2, 1967. About forty fully armed Panthers walked right into the California Assembly while it was in session, protesting a bill that would outlaw carrying loaded weapons in public. All were arrested.

This single act—as ill advised as it may have been—just about made the Panthers a household word overnight.

Wayne Davis, then a special agent assigned to the Washington field office, remembers that "there was a great deal of fear about the Panther philosophy."[25] That fear was focused on the "Huey Newton/Bobby Seale faction out on the west coast that had gone to the state capitol armed."[26] Many in the government saw this as "perhaps the beginning of a breakdown in respect for law enforcement."[27] That was putting it mildly.

Media coverage increased with the almost weekly confrontations between Panthers and the Oakland and other Bay Area police departments.

On October 27, 1967, the Black Panthers collided head-on with the Oakland police. At five o'clock in the morning, Oakland police officers Herbert C. Hearnes and John F. Fuey stopped two Panthers for a routine traffic violation. Huey Newton got out of his car and shooting erupted. Newton was shot four times. He survived, but Officer Fuey was killed at the scene. Officer Hearnes was critically wounded. Newton went to prison.

In spite of the Panthers' obvious propensity for violence and their growing national reputation, the FBI still took no steps to include them as a target in the new COINTELPRO.

Another shoot-out occurred on April 11, 1968. One Oakland squad car was hit with more than 150 rounds. Amazingly, no police officers were killed, but two were wounded. Richard Jensen, one of the injured police officers, remembers the fury of the Panther onslaught: "I had been shot maybe nine different times and they thought I was dead. I wasn't but the firing continued. It was like a war going on. We found out later there was thirteen people shooting at us."[28]

One Panther was killed. Eldridge Cleaver was charged with attempted murder and later fled the country.

A September 27, 1968, memorandum from George C. Moore to W. C.

Sullivan advised of things to come: "The information we are reviewing from our sources concerning activities of the BPP clearly indicates that more violence can be expected from this organization in the immediate future."[29]

By May 1968 the Panthers had been involved in several firefights and countless confrontations with police. They had received tremendous news coverage. They were becoming a black power force in the cities and on the nation's campuses. Panthers had made violent threats against the highest officials in Washington.

The FBI reaction to all of this was curious.

Initially, the San Francisco field office—the office of origin in the Black Panther investigation—resisted the whole idea of selecting the Black Panther party to be a COINTELPRO target. Charles W. Bates, the San Francisco special agent-in-charge—who was later to direct the Patty Hearst investigation—was a man who spoke his mind. He did not feel that a COINTELPRO action against the Panthers would be effective, and he made his views known on more than one occasion. However, in time, the headquarters people prevailed. The Panthers were becoming legendary. The public wanted to know what the FBI was doing about them! The Panthers *had* to be placed on the COINTELPRO target list.

And after all, as always, the director was going to have his way. In a scorching four-page memo dated May 27, 1969, Hoover told the San Francisco field office personnel that their reasoning was "not in line with Bureau objectives as to our responsibilities under the CIP [counterintelligence program]." The San Francisco special agent-in-charge received a full dressing down with closing instructions: "The CIP in the San Francisco office must be reevaluated. During the reevaluation, give thorough consideration to the adequacy of the personnel assigned. Insure that you are utilizing the best personnel available in this program. Advise the Bureau of the results of your reevaluation by June 9, 1969."[30]

In September 1968, J. Edgar Hoover had described the Panthers as "the greatest threat to the internal security of the country."[31]

One of the primary aims of the Black Nationalist Hate Group COINTELPRO was to prevent the unification of the various black nationalist groups into one powerful political force. In the March 4, 1968, memo expanding the COINTELPRO, the director outlined its various goals in exhaustive detail. The prevention of "the coalition of black nationalist groups" was goal number one: A united black nationalist force was the director's greatest fear. Interestingly, in the same memo, goal number three called for the prevention of black violence.[32] In fact, an alarming number of COINTELPRO actions achieved just the opposite result.

It should be noted that not all special agents of field offices necessarily agreed with the Black Hate COINTELPRO methodologies or philosophy. As we have seen, there was considerable resistance to the black nationalist program at the San Francisco office. There is reason to believe that disenchantment existed to some degree at most field offices.

Robert Wall—then a special agent in the Washington, D.C., field office—remembers that, as far as programs like the Black Nationalist program were concerned, "investigations on almost anything done by or for black people could be opened simply by labeling it a Racial Matter."[33] Wall investigated teenagers in Washington who simply wanted city government funds restored in order to provide summer employment for ghetto youths. He investigated black-owned bookstores, the Poor People's March, and other matters that had nothing to do with black extremism, but only with black people.

According to Wall, it was common practice for special agents to scan the local paper and look for any kind of racial incident. When one was found, a call would be quickly made to the local police to verify the details. Then a teletype would be sent to headquarters, advising that the matter was under investigation. Matters like this did not usually become full-fledged COINTELPRO actions, but they do illustrate the type of racial thinking that was present within the bureau from top to bottom.

Wall recalls that while he was a special agent "the appalling racism of the FBI on every level became glaringly apparent to me." As time went on, "it seemed as if every dissident black man was a candidate for investigation."[34]

Regarding the Black Panthers, Wall felt that "it was absurd to investigate hundreds of people whose only connection with the Black Panther Party was that the Party was trying to influence them."[35]

The feelings of Special Agent Wall, and perhaps others like him, had no direct bearing on the investigations or the basic thrust of this COINTELPRO. Hoover's word was the law. Indeed, the actions taken against the black nationalists were probably the most dangerous and aggressive of all the COINTELPROs.

In southern California, the bureau's intent was to promote violence between the Black Panther party and another black group known as the

United Slaves (US) Incorporated. Ostensibly, the effort was to nullify the power of each.

By the fall of 1968 the Panthers were the most widely known and the most widely feared of all the black militant groups in the United States; their membership at this time totaled about 3,000. US, headed by Ron Karenga, was every bit as militant as the Panthers; they wore olive drab uniforms and were trained in karate.

For a time the two groups were allies on a number of projects. Ron Karenga remembers that "we used to do community patrol together."[36]

During the summer of 1968 the San Diego field office conducted interviews of virtually all members of the US group. "In these interviews," a COINTELPRO memorandum of May 31, 1968, notes, "questions will be asked in such a manner as to weaken the influence of leaders of the group." Any group tendency toward dissension was encouraged. By working closely with the San Diego Police Department, the FBI made it difficult for the US group to hold meetings.[37]

By the late fall of 1968 the political landscape had changed. It became clear that the Black Panther–US relationship was in serious trouble. Many members of both groups came from San Diego east-side youth gangs, and they knew the meaning of gang warfare. Both groups wanted to be number one.

A September 25, 1968, COINTELPRO memorandum from the Los Angeles field office told headquarters of the depth of the split between the groups. Several informants reported that the Panthers had "let a contract"[38] on US leader Ron Karenga.

This same memo reported that the Peace and Freedom Party (PFP), which had some white members, was an active financial supporter of the Panthers. Evidently, the Panthers were not impressed with white support. The memo predicted that Caucasians in PFP "will be stood up against the wall with other whites and eliminated."[39] With specific reference to the Panther–US friction, the memo said that "Los Angeles is presently analyzing the situation to determine if further disruption can be caused between these two antagonists."[40]

Black militants' phone calls were being monitored at this time. Not surprisingly, the Los Angeles office was also requesting income tax and selective service records to "determine if a counter-intelligence technique can be used in this regard."[41]

On November 2, 1968, the bureau learned that US members planned to kill Eldridge Cleaver. The next day, at a Black Panther rally in Los

Angeles, a bureau undercover informant learned that a Panther had been revealed as a US informant. The Panthers planned to kill him.[42] Three weeks later, a headquarters memo noted the state of virtual "gang warfare" with "attendant threats of murder and reprisals" between US and the Panthers. "Hard hitting counterintelligence measures aimed at crippling the BPP"[43] were ordered. Threats of violence and provocative surveillance by the two groups continued on a daily basis.

On January 19 a violent clash occurred at the Westwood campus of the University of California at Los Angeles. The Panthers and US members disagreed over the selection process for an Afro-American studies director at the university. Shouting and threats followed. Then, at Campbell Hall located on the campus, a savage firefight broke out. One US member—Larry Stiner—was hit and went down, but survived. Two Panthers—Apprentice "Buckey" Carter and John Huggins—were killed outright. It was later claimed by the Panthers that those who actually did the shooting were FBI agents.

On February 20, 1969, the San Diego field office—in an attempt to maintain and probably exacerbate the tension between the rival groups—requested permission to mail derogatory and highly inflammatory cartoons to the southern California Black Panther offices and to the homes of other Panther leaders across the country.[44] By this time, the FBI was actively investigating all forty-two Panther chapters then known to be in existence, plus more than 1,000 active Panther members. Mailings would be anonymous but made to appear as if they came from the US organization.

Authorization was quickly given on February 27, 1969. The cartoons themselves—extraordinarily crude and abrasive—were mailed during the first week of March 1969. One in particular featured a Panther member hanging from a tree and two smiling US members looking on. The caption read, "He really was a paper tiger." Other cartoons were meant to imply that the entire Panther organization was "riddled with graft and corruption."

The response to the mailing was immediate. A San Diego field office memo dated March 12, 1969, advised that the original mailing was on target.[45] Informants reported that Panther members were outraged. They were indeed fooled into thinking that the mailings were coming from the United Slaves.

Other strategies were also at work.

Around the same time as the cartoon mailing, the San Diego field office placed anonymous calls to Panther members, falsely advising that others in their group were police informants.

The violence continued. On March 17 a Panther member was hit by US gunfire and critically wounded at a rally near Carver High School in Los Angeles. A counterattack followed: Panthers fired several rounds into the home of a US member.

The San Diego FBI office followed up with another mailing of inflammatory materials to Panthers in Sacramento, Los Angeles, and New York.

In April 1969 the bureau mailed out still more crude cartoons that ridiculed Panther members. Again, the illustrations were crude. Continuing a favorite motif, one showed two of the dead Panthers—Huggins and Carter—looked on by gleeful US members. A flyer was sent to the United Slaves (purportedly from the Panthers) that referred to US members as "Pork chop niggers."

On April 4, 1969, there was another confrontation between the two groups, in Southcrest Park in San Diego. According to an FBI undercover informant who was at the scene, the Panthers literally "ran the US members off."[46] On the same day, US members broke into a Panther education meeting and "roughed up" a female Panther member.[47]

A San Diego memo dated April 10, 1969, reported that "the BPP members strongly object to being made fun of by cartoons distributed by the US organization." Informants reported that the continuous mailing of cartoons was "really shaking up the BPP. . . . They have made the BPP feel that US is getting ready to move and this was the cause of the confrontation at Southcrest Park on 4/4/69."[48]

There was more gunfire. On May 23 John Savage, a Panther member, was shot and killed by US member Terry Horne. A June 5, 1969, memo to headquarters reported that the almost daily confrontation between the two groups ranged "from mere harassment up to and including beatings of various individuals."[49] A few days later it was also reported that US members were buying large amounts of ammunition including "9mm, 32 automatic, and 38 special."[50] In this atmosphere of extraordinary tension, the FBI decided to take even more action.

The San Diego field office mailed a forged Black Panther letter to Panther headquarters in Oakland. The letter expressed outrage and dismay over the killing of local Panther members at the hands of the United

Slaves; and in an obvious attempt to create tension within the Panther organization, the letter stated that the local Panther leader had a white girlfriend.

The violence continued. US members shot and wounded two Panthers on August 14, 1969. The next day, US members shot and killed Panther member Sylvester Bell. On August 30, the US office in San Diego was firebombed by retaliating Panthers.

The San Diego FBI office was pleased with these new developments. In a September 18, 1969, memo to bureau headquarters, the field office reported, "In view of the recent killing of BPP member Sylvester Bell, a new cartoon is being considered in the hopes that it will assist in the continuance of the rift between BPP and US." The memo pointed out that "a substantial amount of the unrest is directly attributed to this program."[51]

On November 12, 1969, the San Diego office learned that US leader Ron Karenga feared he would be killed by the Panthers. To heighten this fear, the office sent a letter—anonymous, but appearing to come from a US ally—that strongly suggested that he order reprisals against the Panthers.

On January 29, 1970, new cartoons were approved by headquarters for release by the San Diego, San Francisco, and Los Angeles field offices. One portrayed a Panther leader as basically antagonistic toward black women and children. Another suggested that US leader Ron Karenga had the Panthers completely at his mercy.

On May 2, 1970, an extremely hostile article entitled "KARENGA, KING OF THE BLOOD SUCKERS" appeared in the Black Panther newspaper. Headquarters requested proposals from the field offices to use the article in stirring up even more violence.

The Los Angeles field office replied that it was now difficult to induce Panther members to attack the US group in southern California because the Panthers now feared the United Slaves.

By the end of May 1970, the efforts to promote Panther–US violence had come to a halt. The beatings, the confrontations, the surveillance, the street violence, together with the extremely destructive work of undercover informants, had combined to practically destroy the Panther organization in San Diego and, to a lesser extent, on the entire West Coast. The US group had also suffered. Ron Karenga recalls, "We knew it wasn't going to be a tea party but we didn't anticipate how violent the U.S. government would get."[52]

Discussing the bureau's rather blatant efforts to encourage violence between the groups, the FBI Black Nationalist supervisor later recalled, "You make the best judgment you can based on all the circumstances and you always have an element of doubt where you are dealing with individuals that I think most people would characterize as having a degree of instability."[53]

Another, far less violent COINTELPRO strategy was to create tension and mistrust within the groups, so as to neutralize their effectiveness from the inside.

In several situations, FBI COINTELPRO actions attempted to destroy group members' marriages.

In Saint Louis, a black-nationalist group member's wife—described by friends as an intelligent and respectable woman—received an anonymous bureau letter saying that her husband had "been making it here" with other women in his organization and that "he gives us this jive 'bout their better in bed than you."[54]

In San Francisco, the wife of a Panther leader received an anonymous letter that accused her husband of having affairs with several teenage girls, and taking some of the girls on trips with him.

In another situation in Saint Louis, a husband who had expressed concern about his wife's activities in a biracial group received an anonymous letter that caused him and his wife to separate. The letter said, in part, "Look man. I guess your old lady doesn't get enough at home or she wouldn't be shuckin and jivin with our Black men in this group."[55]

In Chicago another type of internal discord was created. In March 1969, a local Panther leader made known his fears that a party faction led by Fred Hampton and Bobby Rush was "out to get him." The bureau capitalized on the situation by sending an anonymous letter to Fred Hampton in an effort to create additional strain in the Panther's relations with another group—the Blackstone Rangers—and within the Panther group itself. The letter read, "Brother Hampton: Just a word of warning. A Stone friend tells me [name deleted] wants the Panthers and is looking for somebody to get you out of the way. Brother Jeff [leader of the Blackstone Rangers] is supposed to be interested. I'm just a black man looking for blacks working together, not more of this gang banging."[56]

The FBI Key Black Extremist Program which was incorporated into the COINTELPRO strategy, began in 1970. Key black extremists were defined as "black activists who were particularly agitative, extreme, and vocal in their demands for terrorism and violence."[57] Reports on these extremists were to be submitted every ninety days.

One of the bureau's most successful efforts at creating internal strife within the Black Panthers played on the schism that had developed between the followers of Eldridge Cleaver and those who followed Huey Newton. This program began in March 1970 while Cleaver was in exile in Algeria and Newton was in prison. An anonymous bureau letter was sent to Cleaver in Algeria to tell him that certain Panther officials in California were actively working against him. The letter was a master-piece of deceit. Cleaver responded immediately by expelling three leaders from the party, and a furious exchange of letters between Panther leaders in California and Cleaver soon followed.

On August 13, 1970, Huey Newton was released from prison. The Philadelphia Panther office, as well as the national headquarters, received an anonymous bureau letter questioning Newton's competence and leadership.

FBI wiretaps at Panther headquarters and at other offices, together with informant reporting, confirmed that the anonymous letters were very unsettling to the party as a whole.

In the summer of 1970 Cleaver led a delegation to North Vietnam and North Korea. A letter was sent to Cleaver, criticizing Newton for not having arranged adequate press coverage.

In January 1971 an anonymous letter to Cleaver—written to appear as if it had come from Connie Matthews, Newton's secretary—read, in part,

> Things around headquarters are dreadfully disorganized with the comrade commander not making proper decisions. The newspaper is in a shambles. No one knows who is in charge. The foreign department gets no support. . . . I fear there is rebellion working just beneath the surface. . . .
>
> We must either get rid of the Supreme Commander [Newton] or get rid of the disloyal members.[58]

On January 28, 1971, bureau headquarters announced that Newton had immediately disciplined several Panther leaders. Newton had said emphatically that he was prepared to "respond violently to any question of his actions or policies."[59]

On February 2, a bureau memo asked the field offices for still more proposals aimed at causing even more dissension within the Panthers.

The memo said in part that "dissension coupled with financial difficulties offers an exceptional opportunity to further disrupt, aggravate, and possibly neutralize this organization through counterintelligence."[60]

Almost immediately, twenty-nine FBI field offices fired off a withering barrage of acrimonious letters to top-level Panthers. In this campaign, letters reached Eldridge Cleaver, Kathleen Cleaver, Huey Newton, Melvin Newton, David Hilliard, and a number of others on both sides of the Newton–Cleaver divide. Kathleen Cleaver later recalled that "we did not know who to believe about what, so the general effect, not only of the letters but of the whole situation in which the letters were a part was creating uncertainty. It was a very bizarre feeling."[61]

Thus, this mailing campaign too came to a close. The bureau concluded in a March 25, 1971, memo that "since the differences between Newton and Cleaver now appear to be irreconcilable, no further counterintelligence activity in this regard will be undertaken at this time and now new targets must be established."[62]

The snitch-jacket technique was another particularly unpleasant COINTELPRO method of creating internal dissension within the Black Panther party. The snitch jacket involved falsely labeling certain innocent Panther members as police informants—or as "snitches"—so that those persons could no longer be trusted by anyone within the Panther organization. A very unpleasant experience.

The methods for creating snitch-jacket rumors varied. In some situations, rumors were started by using falsified informants' reports; in others, anonymous phone calls or letters to key Panthers were used; in still other situations, actual informants themselves were used to create snitch-jacket rumors.

In one situation in San Diego, a Black Panther leader and four members were arrested. The four members were released by police in a few days, but the leader remained in custody. The Panthers wanted to know why. The bureau authorized the San Diego office to circulate the rumor that their leader had not been released because "he is cooperating with and has made a deal with the Los Angeles Police Department to furnish them with information about the BPP."[63] All of this was completely untrue.

Nevertheless, this Panther's career—that is, *if* he managed to escape violence at the hands of the other Panthers—was all but finished. In this situation—to make matters even worse—after he was released he received an anonymous bureau phone call advising him that his arrest had been caused by a rival black leader.

The New York field office learned that the chairman of the New York Black Panther Party was suspected of being an informant—which he was not. In any event, the suspicion stemmed from the arrest of another Panther member on a weapons charge. The FBI saw an opportunity here and decided to "cast further suspicion on him." The bureau sent anonymous letters to the wife of the arrested member, to a number of other black groups in New York, and to Panther officials throughout the state. The letter said, "Danger Beware—Black Brothers, [target name deleted] is the fink who told the pigs that [arrested Panther name deleted] were carrying guns."[64] The letter even furnished the targeted Panther's home address.

In a volatile situation in Newark, New Jersey, the bureau determined the hiding place of a Panther fugitive by means of a telephone tap. Then, after the Panther's arrest, the bureau attempted to create as much distrust and disruption as possible within the Panther organization. This finger-pointing letter was sent to the captured Panther's brother.

Brother:

Jimmie was sold out by Sister [name deleted—the BPP leader who made the phone call picked up by the tap] for some pig money to pay her rent. When she don't get it that way she takes Panther money. How come her kid sells the paper in his school and no one bothers him. How comes Tyler got busted up by the pigs and her kid didn't. How comes the FBI pig fascists knew where to bust Lonnie and Winnie way out where they were.

—Think baby[65]

Another snitch-jacket operation developed in March 1971 in Charlotte, North Carolina. An important local Panther official had been photographed outside of a house where Panthers had held a shoot-out with local police. The photograph showed the snitch-jacket target talking to a police officer. The photo, together with newspaper copy and an accompanying handwritten note, was sent to Panther headquarters in Oakland, California. The letter, allegedly from a disenchanted female Panther, said that "I think this is the pigs oinking."[66]

In all, the snitch-jacket technique was used in at least a dozen different field offices during the life of the Black Nationalist Hate Group COINTELPRO. In most cases, the damage to the credibility of individual Panthers was simply beyond repair.

George Moore, racial intelligence chief within the bureau during these years, later recalled, "You have to be able to make decisions and I am sure that labeling somebody as an informant, that you'd want to make certain that it served a good purpose before you did it and not do it haphazardly. It is a serious thing. As far as I am aware, in the black extremist area, by using that technique [the snitch-jacket] no one was killed. I am sure of that." Moore was asked whether the fact that no one was killed was just a matter of luck. He answered, "Oh, it just happened that way, I'm sure."[67]

Other former COINTELPRO supervisors do not agree. One in particular said that the labeling of Panthers as informants almost certainly led to violence and injury or death.

As part of the overall Black Nationalist operation, the FBI did not hesitate to take COINTELPRO actions against the black clergy and church organizations that funded black nationalist activities.

Donald W. Jackson, a black minister from Chester, Pennsylvania became a target of the bureau. Jackson, originally an antipoverty worker in the Chester area, changed his name to Muhammad Kenyatta before moving to Jackson, Mississippi. In 1969 Kenyatta was a college student at Tougaloo College in Mississippi. He was also involved with the Jackson Human Rights Project, which was funded by the Episcopal church.

The bureau watched Kenyatta closely. A Jackson, Mississippi, field office memo of February 26, 1969, advised that "Jackson [Kenyatta] gave an inflammatory anti-white, anti-establishment and anti–law enforcement speech and told the crowd that the FBI had informants at Tougaloo College."[68]

The memo said that Kenyatta was one of four instructors at the Black and Proud School in Jackson.[69] An April 16, 1969, memo reported that Kenyatta had been dismissed from college because of unpaid bills, that he had attempted to steal a television set from the college, and that he and some of his associates were involved in several acts of wild and disruptive behavior during Black Spring Weekend, which took place on the Tougaloo campus during April 10–13, 1969.[70]

The Jackson field office, with approval from bureau headquarters, prepared the letter below. It was mailed to Kenyatta on April 25, 1969.

Muhammad Kenyatta—

The deplorable activities and conduct of you and your Black Panther brothers at the recently completed Black Spring Weekend have shocked the Tougaloo College community into realizing the basic errors in the intimidation methods and nihilistic doctrines which you promote. Your immature actions of discharging firearms near the campus on Saturday afternoon, April 11, further alienated you and your "outsiders" from the spirit and tone in which all desired the BSW to take. Your recent involvement in various criminal activities in and near Tougaloo College as well as your irresponsibility in paying your school bills while at Tougaloo College further exemplify the inappropriateness of you, of all people, in any manner acting as a representative of blacks in Mississippi or anywhere for that matter. Your conduct and demeanor is representative of traits and habits we in our quest are trying to rise above.

Accordingly, it has been determined by solidly representative elements of the Tougaloo College Student Body that you are directed to remain away from this campus until such time as your conduct and general demeanor reach the desired level. This directive also applies to your bringing any of your unruly and undisciplined associates to the campus.

Should you feel that this is a hollow directive and not heed our diplomatic and well thought out warning we shall consider contacting local authorities regarding some of your activities or take other measures available to us which would have a more direct effect and which would not be as cordial as this note.

Tougaloo College Defense Committee[71]

The letter had an immediate impact. Kenyatta moved to Philadelphia very soon thereafter.

On May 24 a representative of the Episcopal church contacted the Jackson FBI field office. Rumors about Kenyatta's behavior had reached him; he was looking for updated information on Kenyatta and the Jackson Human Rights Project. The bureau, as might be imagined, was happy to oblige the church representative. The FBI referred him to several sources that, according to a May 27, 1969, Jackson field office memo, "were in possession of or contained derogatory information regarding Kenyatta to include arrests, affiliation with black extremist groups, and unfavorable publicity received from his attempted 'take-over' of church meetings and services in Pennsylvania and elsewhere."[72]

The church was not happy with what was found. In August 1969 the FBI field office announced to bureau headquarters that "funds previously approved for [the] Jackson Human Rights Project have been discontinued . . . due to the development of derogatory information regarding Mr. Kenyatta's activities."[73]

The FBI made a number of additional attempts to stop sources from funding targeted black nationalist organizations. The New York office learned from an undercover informant that the Student Non-violent Coordinating Committee was attempting to obtain about $35,000 in funds from the Episcopal church. The money would finance SNCC's planned "liberation school." The FBI used a series of well-placed anonymous derogatory letters alleging that SNCC was really planning to use the money for a "fraudulent scheme." The SNCC also anticipated funding from the Inter-religious Foundation for Community Organization to finance various social reform plans. Again the bureau took action. In this situation, an anonymous letter to the potential funding organization suggested that the funds would really be used by SNCC in an "illegal kickback scheme."[74]

In Pittsburgh a black nationalist group known as Unity, Incorporated, was working to obtain a $150,000 grant from the Mellon Foundation. Unity operated a black power center in Pittsburgh and planned, among other things, to build a target range in their headquarters basement. The FBI, alerted to this situation, developed a contact inside the Mellon organization. The bureau apprised the organization of the true nature of Unity, Incorporated. The funding was quickly blocked. A COINTEL-PRO memo dated August 28, 1968, from the Pittsburgh field office advised headquarters that "it can be stated with certainty that Unity, Inc. did not receive a grant from the Mellon Foundation because of this counterintelligence operation."[75]

In twenty-six separate COINTELPRO actions, the bureau made information "available to friendly media representatives for the purpose of using such material in a newspaper, magazine, or radio or television program to expose and make public the objectives and activities of the Black Panther Party"[76] and other black nationalist hate groups. In all cases, this information was supplied to the media on the basis that the source would never be revealed.

The bureau's use of news information, which was administered by the Crime Records Division, was handled in two different ways: first, by placing negative information or propaganda about the Panthers and other black *organizations* with the news media and, second, by leaking derogatory information intended to discredit particular *individuals* within black organizations.

Internal memoranda that dealt specifically with using the media for COINTELPRO operations were labeled within the bureau as part of the Mass Media Program. The Crime Records Division disseminated media information at the request of the Domestic Intelligence Division.

In Tampa, information on an extremist group known as the Junta of Military Organizations was furnished to a friendly contact at a local television station. The local station manager, of course, had no idea that this particular black group was a COINTELPRO target. After the information had been used by the station, several special agents were invited to see a preview of the half-hour show. According to a Tampa field office memo dated February 7, 1969, the Tampa special agent-in-charge complimented the station manager on his work. The special agent also suggested that the program should be shown to civic groups in the area. A headquarters memo in early spring of that year congratulated the Tampa office on a job well done.

Miami television station WCKT-TV made several television documentaries based on information secretly supplied by the FBI, including one on black nationalist extremist groups in 1968. The thirty-minute program appeared on WCKT-TV on Sunday evening, July 7, 1968, at 6:30 P.M. The audience was estimated at 250,000 viewers. It was rated as one of the "week's best" by a local newspaper. J. Edgar Hoover narrated the end of the program.

A COINTELPRO memo from Hoover dated August 5, 1968, was sent to all COINTELPRO participating field offices. It praised the work of the Miami field office. "Miami has demonstrated," it said, "that a carefully planned television show can be extremely effective in showing these extremists for what they are." Hoover mentioned that "the interviewer of black nationalist leaders on the show had the leaders seated, ill at ease, in hard chairs. Full-length camera shots showed each movement as they squirmed about in their chairs, resembling rats trapped under scientific observation." The director concluded by strongly suggesting that "each office should be alert to the possibility of using this technique."[77]

In San Francisco, a special agent assigned to monitor the bank account of Eldridge Cleaver learned that Kathleen Cleaver withdrew $33,000 in cash in December 1968. The FBI quickly leaked this information to the local press, and it appeared in print almost immediately. To add additional weight to the story it was "backed up by a statement from the office of the U.S. attorney verifying the accuracy of the account." Kathleen Cleaver reacted strongly. She held a news conference on December 23, 1968, and "claimed that the story was an FBI plot to discredit her husband and the BPP."[78]

The damage, however, had already been done. Informants reported that publicity regarding the huge cash withdrawal was beginning to cause the Black Panther party considerable fund-raising difficulties.

In January 1970, apparently in an effort to duplicate the success of the Miami program, a memo was directed to nine selected field offices. Special agents were again instructed to contact any reliable connections in the television and/or radio field who might be interested in drawing up a program for local consumption, depicting the true facts regarding the BPP.[79]

In July 1970 a bureau-backed editorial appeared on television in the Los Angeles area. Other features soon followed. All were sharply critical of the Panthers and other black extremist groups.[80]

In February 1971 an article appeared in the *San Francisco Examiner* that was based on bureau-supplied information. It reported that the supreme commander of the Black Panther party, Huey Newton, was living in a lavish apartment overlooking Lake Merritt in Oakland under the assumed name of Don Penn. Copies of the article were forwarded to bureau offices and Panther chapters nationwide.[81]

The Memphis, Tennessee, field office also worked closely with local media. A 1970 field office memo told FBI headquarters that the "leaking of derogatory information regarding the Invaders [a Memphis-area black nationalist group] and their plans to a trusted newspaper source has resulted in almost daily articles exposing the activities of the militant group."[82]

The Memphis special agent-in-charge stated that, according to informants, the articles in the newspaper had disillusioned many in the Memphis black community. Interestingly, a number of Memphis merchants who had been extortion targets of the Invaders were now ready to come forward and testify. Indeed, a number of blacks said that they now wanted to work in cooperation with the Memphis Police Department.

Some COINTELPRO actions were developed specifically to prevent black extremist–group officials from speaking at public forums.

In Chicago the FBI, working through an undercover informant, learned that Chicago Black Panther leader Fred Hampton was scheduled to appear on a local talk show. The bureau knew that a warrant had been issued for Hampton in the Chicago area and it had not yet been served. A golden opportunity fell into the bureau's hands: Chicago police served Hampton's arrest warrant right in the television studio in front of about twenty-five fellow Panther members and studio personnel just before air time. In February 1969 bureau headquarters congratulated the Chicago field office for the timing of the arrest "under circumstances which proved highly embarrassing to the BPP."[83]

Another important disruption involved Panther official Bobby Seale. Seale had planned to make an extensive speaking tour on the West Coast to raise badly needed operating funds for the Panther organization. He arrived in Oregon in May 1969. On the eve of his first speech, the FBI anonymously telephoned Seale's mother and advised her that her son would not be safe. Mrs. Seale immediately telephoned Panther officials in Oakland, who took the matter very seriously. A portion of Seale's fund raising, including a major trip to Seattle, was cancelled. The San Francisco field office estimated that, as a result of the cancellations, the Panthers lost more than $1,700.

The bureau's overall program to neutralize black groups also included efforts to undermine groups and celebrities who supported them. Leonard Bernstein—for example—became a target, as did Jane Fonda. An FBI anonymous letter to Hollywood gossip columnist Army Archerd advised that Jane Fonda had appeared at a Panther fund-raising event. And in at least one instance, the bureau's efforts to neutralize a Panther supporter turned out tragically.

Jean Seberg, a white Hollywood actress, was probably at the peak of her acting career in 1970. She was also a supporter of the Black Panthers, and as such she became a COINTELPRO target.

In April 1970, Seberg was pregnant and married to the French author and diplomat Romain Gary. The bureau decided to neutralize her. An FBI memo written in the spring of 1970 stated, "Jean Seberg has been a financial supporter of the BPP and should be neutralized. Her current pregnancy by [name deleted] while still married affords an opportunity for such effort."[84]

As the result of an anonymous FBI news release to the *Los Angeles Times* gossip columnist Joyce Harber, a lengthy column appeared about

Seberg—referred to as "Miss A"—in which the suggestion was made that the father was a Black Panther.

The column closed by saying, "According to those really international sources Topic A is the baby Miss A is expecting and its father. Papa's said to be a rather prominent Black Panther."[85] The effect on the actress was traumatic. Seberg's husband reported that she immediately went into labor. The child, a girl, was delivered by emergency caesarean section and died three days later.

Gary reported that the emotional damage to Seberg was devastating. She attempted to commit suicide every year thereafter on the anniversary of the child's death. She succeeded on September 8, 1979. Fifteen months later Romain Gary, her former husband, also ended his own life.

Joyce Harber, the *Los Angeles Times* columnist who wrote the Jean Seberg story, has since left the *Times*. She recalls, "If I was used by the FBI, I didn't know it. To my knowledge, I didn't know anyone with the FBI then, and I don't now."[86]

Other tragedies resulted from the COINTELPRO.

In Chicago, as in almost all major cities with Panther chapters, bureau informants were placed in important positions.

In 1968 Chicago special agent Ray M. Mitchell recruited William O'Neal and several other blacks to infiltrate the local Panther chapter. O'Neal, a nineteen-year-old who was recruited while serving a jail term, remembers, "Mitchell asked me to join the Black Panther Party. He never used the word 'informant.' He always said, 'You are working for me.' "

O'Neal was well paid and was very successful. He quickly moved up the ranks to become chief of security and a personal bodyguard to Fred Hampton, vice-chairman of the Chicago chapter. O'Neal began his work as an undercover informant in 1968 and, by the fall of 1969, it was evident that the bureau's pressure was mounting.[87] Around this time, in fact, the Chicago police along with the bureau were watching the Panthers very closely. There were periodic confrontations and several raids on Panther facilities. On October 20, 1969, J. Edgar Hoover advised Attorney General John N. Mitchell of the results obtained from the FBI telephone surveillance then in operation at the Chicago office of the Panthers, located at 2350 West Madison Street.[88] The FBI learned for example that instructions and directions came from Panther headquarters in Berkeley, California. Information was also received concerning firefights between the Panthers and the Chicago police in July and October of 1969. The surveillance revealed that the Panthers planned to retaliate against the Chicago police for the October raid of the Panther office.

O'Neal later said, "Within the Panther organization, it was a given—that we would have wiretaps, that we would be followed, that we would be harassed."[89]

On November 13 there was a firefight between Chicago police and Panther Jake Winters. Two police officers were killed; shock waves went through the city.

O'Neal remembers, "The shoot-out on the South Side had pretty much laid the foundation within the party, within the Black Panthers. We knew the police would react in some type of way. . . . We knew something bad was going to happen."[90]

The FBI intensified its surveillance.

On November 19, O'Neal informed Special Agent Mitchell that the Panthers were stockpiling weapons at a first-floor apartment located at 2337 West Monroe. The inventory included carbines, shotguns, revolvers, smoke bombs, and more than 50,000 rounds of ammunition.

Four days later, on November 23, 1969, O'Neal advised that the Panthers somehow knew that Chicago Police Gang Intelligence Unit planned to raid the Panthers' weapons supply. The raid was canceled. The weapons were moved to another location.

On December 1, the bureau learned that the weapons had been moved back to the West Monroe location. O'Neal gave Mitchell a detailed inventory of the weapons, a floor plan of the West Monroe Street apartment showing where Panther Vice-chairman Hampton slept, and a list of all the Panthers who lived there. On December 2, Special Agent Mitchell gave this information to Assistant State Attorney Richard Jalovec and Cook County State Attorney Edward V. Hanrahan.

A raid was authorized. It was to be led by Police Sergeant Daniel Groth of the Chicago Police Department.

The police squad—nine white and five black officers—arrived at Panther headquarters at 4:45 A.M. on December 4. Ostensibly they were there to serve a warrant and conduct a search. What happened next has been the subject of much debate. Sergeant Groth has said that they were fired upon first and they returned the fire.[91]

Deborah Johnson, a twenty-one-year-old Panther at the time, remembers a night of complete terror. She recalls that a Panther came running into Hampton's bedroom screaming, "Chairman, Chairman, wake up, the pigs are back."[92] At that point there was a complete fire storm. Police fired almost 100 rounds. Fred Hampton was hit twice in the head, once in the arm and shoulder. He died, as did his associate Mark Clark. Seven survived the raid. The Chicago chapter, for all practical purposes, had been destroyed.

On June 20, 1970, the Detroit field office, which had planted several informants in the local Panther chapter, was informed that the Panthers were planning to ambush several Detroit police officers on the city's east side. The FBI immediately notified the Detroit Police Department.

On June 27, informants further detailed the exact time and place of the ambush. The next day the attempted ambush and accompanying firefight did occur. The Panthers were surrounded and a total of eight were ultimately arrested; a huge arsenal of weapons and ammunition, together with fifty sticks of dynamite, was captured.

As with other COINTELPROs, the Black Nationalist Hate Group campaign came to a rather abrupt end, on April 28, 1971.

In total, bureau headquarters had received 540 COINTELPRO proposals from forty-one approved field offices. Of these, 302 actions were implemented, with known results obtained in seventy-six separate actions. The Black Panther party was the primary target.

The bureau had again used its extraordinary range of counterintelligence tools. The technique of sending anonymous or fictitious materials to members or groups to create discord and friction was used repeatedly with fatal consequences. A number of black extremists were killed in street violence as a direct result of bureau actions.

In twenty-six cases, public source material was made available to media contacts; one-seventh of the Black Hate COINTELPRO actions involved leaking nonpublic information to friendly media. Undercover extremist informants were used in almost all Black Nationalist actions. In seven cases, employers and creditors were advised of individual Black Panther party-member activity; in sixty-two cases, the bureau "notified persons or businesses with whom members had economic dealings of the member's association with the various groups involved for the purpose of adversely affecting their economic interests."[93] In thirty-six situations, the FBI attempted to use religious or civic leaders to disrupt Black Panther activities. In twelve COINTELPRO actions, family members or friends were advised of Panther activities.

In many areas, the Black Panthers and other black extremist groups were decimated. A number of individuals were killed. In a number of situations, constitutional guarantees were clearly violated. William C. Sullivan—former assistant to the director—said, when referring to the COINTELPRO programs, "This is a rough, tough, dirty business, and dangerous."[94]

Indeed, how right he was.

NOTES

1. Theodore White, *The Making of the President 1968* (New York: Atheneum Publishers, 1969), pp. 25–27.

2. Ibid., pp. 23–30, 188–223.

3. Ibid., p. 200.

4. Senate Select Committee to Study Governmental Operations with Respect to Intelligence Activities, "Intelligence Activities and the Rights of Americans," Book II, 94th Cong., 2d sess., 14 Apr. 1976, p. 61.

5. Senate Select Committee to Study Governmental Operations with Respect to Intelligence Activities, "FBI Intelligence and the Black Community," Book II, 94th Cong., 2d sess., 14 Apr. 1976, pp. 475–91.

6. Ibid.

7. Kenneth O'Reilly, *Racial Matters: The FBI's Secret War on Black America, 1966–1972* (New York: Free Press, 1990), pp. 268–69.

8. Senate Select Committee, "Intelligence Activities and the Rights of Americans," Book II, p. 83.

9. Lyndon B. Johnson, *The Vantage Point: Prospectives of the Presidency, 1963–1969* (New York: Holt, Rinehart & Winston, 1971), pp. 167–68.

10. White, *Making of the President 1968*, pp. 23–30, 188–223.

11. The President's Address to the Nation on Civil Disorders, Public Papers of Presidents, Lyndon Baines Johnson Foundation, Austin, Texas, 27 July 1967, 2:721.

12. FBI Memorandum, Headquarters to Field Offices, 25 Aug. 1967.

13. Ibid.

14. Ibid.

15. Ibid.

16. Senate Select Committee, "Intelligence Activities and the Rights of Americans," Book II, p. 21.

17. O'Reilly, *Racial Matters*, p. 265.

18. Senate Select Committee, "Intelligence Activities and the Rights of Americans," Book II, p. 75.

19. Senate Select Committee to Study Governmental Operations with Respect to Intelligence Activities, Book III, 94th Cong., 2d sess. 14 Apr. 1976, p. 493.

20. O'Reilly, *Racial Matters*, p. 269.

21. FBI Memorandum, Headquarters to Field Offices, 4 Mar. 1968.

22. FBI Memorandum, Headquarters to FBI Field Offices, 3 Apr. 1968.

23. Henry Hampton, Steve Fayer, and Sarah Flynn, *Voices of Freedom: An Oral History of the Civil Rights Movement from the 1950's through the 1980's* (New York: Bantam Books, 1989), p. 351.

24. Ibid., p. 353.

25. Ibid., p. 512.

26. Ibid., p. 513.

27. Ibid.

28. Hampton, Fayer, and Flynn, *Voices of Freedom*, p. 516.

29. FBI Memorandum, George C. Moore to W. C. Sullivan, 27 Sept. 1968.

30. FBI Memorandum, Headquarters to San Francisco Field Office, 27 May 1969.

31. O'Reilly, *Racial Matters*, p. 297.

32. FBI Memorandum, Headquarters to Field Offices, 4 Mar. 1968.

33. Robert Wall, "Special Agent for the FBI," *New York Times Book Review*, 27 Jan. 1972, pp. 16–17.

34. Ibid., p. 17.

35. Ibid., p. 18.

36. O'Reilly, *Racial Matters*, p. 305.

37. FBI Memorandum, San Diego Field Office to Headquarters, 25 September 1968.

38. FBI Memorandum, Los Angeles Field Office to Headquarters, 25 September 1968.

39. Ibid.

40. Ibid.

41. Ibid.

42. FBI Memorandum, George C. Moore to W. C. Sullivan, 5 Nov. 1968.

43. FBI Memorandum, Headquarters to Baltimore Field Office, 25 Nov. 1968.

44. FBI Memorandum, San Diego Field Office to Headquarters, 20 Feb. 1969.

45. FBI Memorandum, San Diego Field Office to Headquarters, 12 Mar. 1969.

46. FBI Memorandum, San Diego Field Office to Headquarters, 10 Apr. 1969.

47. Ibid.

48. Ibid.

49. FBI Memorandum, San Diego Field Office to Headquarters, 5 June 1969.

50. FBI Memorandum, San Diego Field Office to Headquarters, 13 June 1969.

51. FBI Memorandum, San Diego Field Office to Headquarters, 18 Sept. 1969.

52. O'Reilly, *Racial Matters*, p. 309.

53. Senate Select Committee, Book III, p. 40.

54. Ibid., p. 55.

55. Ibid., p. 53.

56. FBI Memorandum, Headquarters to Chicago Field Office, 8 Apr. 1969.

57. Senate Select Committee, Book III, pp. 517–18.

58. FBI Memorandum, San Francisco Field Office to Headquarters, 18 Jan. 1970.

59. FBI Memorandum, Headquarters to Boston, New York, Los Angeles, and San Francisco Field Offices, 28 Jan. 1971.

60. FBI Memorandum, Headquarters to Twenty-nine Field Offices, 2 Feb. 1971.

61. Senate Select Committee to Study Governmental Operations with Respect to Intelligence Activities, "The FBI's Covert Action Program to Destroy the Black Panther Party," Book III, 94th Cong., 2d sess., 14 Apr. 1976, see Kathleen Cleaver Testimony, 8 Apr. 1976, at p. 34.

62. FBI Memorandum, Headquarters to San Francisco and Chicago Field Offices, 25 Mar. 1971.

63. Senate Select Committee, "FBI's Covert Action Program to Destroy Black Panther Party," Book III, p. 46.

64. FBI Memorandum, New York Field Office to Headquarters, 14 Feb. 1969; FBI Memorandum, Headquarters to New York Field Office, 10 Mar. 1969.

65. FBI Memorandum, Headquarters to Newark Field Office, 3 July 1969; FBI Memorandum, Headquarters to Newark Field Office, 14 July 1969.

66. FBI Memorandum, Charlotte Field Office to Headquarters, 23 Mar. 1971; FBI Memorandum, Headquarters to Charlotte Field Office, 31 Mar. 1971.

67. Senate Select Committee to Study Governmental Operations with Respect to Intelligence Activities, "George C. Moore Testimony, 3 Nov. 1975," Book III, 94th Cong., 2d sess., 14 Apr. 1976, at p. 49.

68. FBI Memorandum, Jackson Field Office to Headquarters, 26 Feb. 1969.

69. Ibid.

70. FBI Memorandum, Jackson Field Office to Headquarters, 16 Apr. 1969.

71. FBI Memorandum, Jackson Field Office to Headquarters, 27 May 1969.

72. Ibid.

73. John M. Crewdson, "Black Pastor Got FBI Threat in '69," *New York Times*, 15 Feb. 1975, p. 1.

74. Senate Select Committee, "The FBI's Action Programs Against American Citizens," Book III, p. 56.

75. FBI Memorandum, Pittsburgh Field Office to Headquarters, 28 Aug. 1968.

76. House Committee on the Judiciary, Civil Rights and Constitutional Rights Subcommittee, *Hearings on FBI Counterintelligence Programs*, 93rd Cong., 2d sess., 20 Nov. 1974, Serial No. 55, p. 13.

77. FBI Memorandum, Headquarters to Field Offices, 5 Aug. 1968.

78. FBI Memorandum, San Francisco Field Office to Headquarters, 30 Dec. 1968.

79. FBI Memorandum, Headquarters to Selected Field Offices, 23 Jan. 1970.

80. FBI Memorandum, Los Angeles Field Office to Headquarters, 10 Sept. 1970.

81. FBI Memorandum, San Francisco Field Office to Headquarters, 12 Feb. 1971.

82. FBI Memorandum, Memphis Field Office to Headquarters, Mar. 1970.

83. FBI Memorandum, Headquarters to Chicago Field Office, 20 Feb. 1969.

84. FBI Memorandum, Headquarters to Los Angeles Field Office, May 1970; Joyce Harber, "Miss A Rates as Expectant Mother," *Los Angeles Times*, 19 May 1970, p. 11.

85. Harber, "Miss A Rates as Expectant Mother," p. 11.

86. Wendell Rawls, Jr., "FBI Admits Planting a Rumor to Discredit Jean Seberg in 1970," *New York Times*, 15 Sept. 1979, p. 1.

87. John Kifner, "Panther Chief of Security Was Paid FBI Informer," *New York Times*, 13 Feb. 1974, p. 18.

88. FBI Memorandum, J. Edgar Hoover for the Attorney General, 20 Oct. 1969.

89. Hampton, Fayer, and Flynn, *Voices of Freedom*, pp. 523–37.

90. Ibid.

91. Andrew M. Malcolm, "Chicago Witness Says Weapons Were Seized in Panther Raid," *New York Times*, 16 July 1972, p. 31.

92. "Survivor Recalls Raid on Panthers," *New York Times*, 23 July 1972.

93. House Civil Rights and Constitutional Rights Subcommittee, *Hearings on FBI Counterintelligence Programs*, p. 13.

94. Senate Select Committee, Book III, p. 7.

6 The New Left COINTELPRO

After the Columbia riot the New Left was fair game.
William C. Sullivan

The year 1968 was one of the most turbulent of this century. It was the year of the assassinations of Robert F. Kennedy and Martin Luther King, the latter of which triggered furious black violence that struck more than 100 cities across the nation.

U.S. troop levels in Vietnam—twenty-three years after the first American serviceman had been killed there—stood at more than 500,000. The prestige of the presidency was at a low ebb. Lyndon Johnson could not travel safely anywhere in the United States.

The forces of violence and protest in the land appeared to be, for all practical purposes, out of control. This same year—1968—reflected, in Theodore White's phrase, "a crisis in the American culture."[1]

On April 23, 1968, the largely white, middle-class Students for a Democratic Society (SDS), along with members of the Afro-American Society, seized Hamilton Hall, the main classroom building at Columbia University. Then they captured Acting University Under-graduate Dean Henry S. Colemon; and then, with virtually no one to stop them, they seized four more campus buildings, including the office of Columbia

University President Grayson Kirk. Kirk's office was destroyed. Students and faculty were barred by the SDS from university classroom buildings, and mobs roamed the campus. A large picture of Karl Marx was placed atop one building. News coverage was extensive.

The radicals were there primarily to protest the war in Vietnam.

On April 29 the university administration had had enough. Police stormed the campus and arrested more than 700 students. More than 100 police officers and students were injured. Three weeks later, more violence erupted at Columbia.

In that strange and violent year, student protest occurred in the streets of Chicago, at Oberlin College, Ohio University, the University of Wisconsin, and the City College of New York. However, the high-water mark—the protest that captured the nation's attention—was the occupation of Columbia University.

William C. Sullivan, then assistant FBI director, remembers being caught completely off guard by the Columbia University occupation. "Before we read the headlines and saw the pictures of Mark Rudd [the SDS campus president at Columbia] smoking a cigar with his feet up on Grayson Kirk's desk we didn't know the New Left existed," he remembers. According to Sullivan, the bureau took the matter "very seriously." The New Left became "fair game."[2]

The Students for a Democratic Society had been founded at Port Huron, Michigan, in June 1962. The Port Huron Statement, written by Tom Hayden, was generally considered to be the manifesto for the SDS: "As a social system we seek the establishment of a democracy of individual participation, governed by two central aims: that the individual share in those social decisions determining the quality and direction of his life; that society be organized to encourage independence in men and provide the media for their common participation."[3]

The first use of the expression "New Left" predated the Port Huron statement by about six months. The New Left called for an evolution—rather than a revolution—in American politics. Those who comprised the New Left saw themselves as basically distinct from the "old left": the Communist Party U.S.A., and the Socialist Workers party.

In the beginning, the New Left was spearheaded mainly by the SDS. The first New Left cause concerned civil rights. In the brutal summer of 1964 the young people of the New Left, as we have seen, saw the horror of racial hatred in Mississippi and other parts of the South. In the same year the New Left was involved in the rioting at the University of California at Berkeley—the first full-scale confrontation between elements of the movement and police. The basic issue in the early Berkeley confrontation was student freedom and, more specifically, free speech.

By 1965 the movement's focus had shifted almost entirely to all-out opposition to the war in Vietnam. The SDS invited anyone who opposed the war—black or white—to join forces in the New Left. At this point the SDS itself, still the leading force within the New Left, had grown to more than 100 chapters nationwide.

The New Left movement grew more and more heterogeneous as it took under its umbrella the Congress of Racial Equality, the Socialist Workers Party, the Communist Party U.S.A., the Student Non-violent Coordinating Committee, the Urban League, the Student Peace Union, the NAACP, the National Mobilization Committee to End the War in Vietnam, the Black Student Union, the Black Panther Party, the Black Student Alliance, the Youth International Party, the Vietnam Day Committee, the Progressive Labor Party, the Vietnam Moratorium Committee, and roughly two dozen more organizations. All were united in one common purpose: to end the war in Vietnam.

The American bombing of North Vietnam began in early 1965. Almost immediately thereafter, "teach-ins" on the subject of why the United States was in Vietnam began to spread to colleges and universities across the country.

The administration was stunned.

The Johnson administration and the FBI took notice of the teach-ins. Thirteen bureau undercover agents attended one in May 1967 sponsored by the Universities Committee on Problems of War and Peace. Members of the SDS, the Young Socialist Alliance, the W.E.B. Du Bois clubs, and many others were identified by name and political affiliation. Also, the names of twenty-three speakers, including university instructors and members of the clergy, were identified. These data were quickly forwarded to headquarters for review, analysis, and placement in the appropriate FBI counterintelligence files. The first FBI report on this event totaled forty-one pages. Copies were sent to the White House, to the Justice Department's Internal Security and Civil Rights Divisions, and to military intelligence. There seems little doubt that President Johnson read the report.

The president was deeply disturbed by the growing antiwar sentiment in the nation. An April 1965 march on Washington by more than 25,000 antiwar activists did not escape his attention. The teach-ins puzzled and angered him. Johnson initially felt that the Communist Party U.S.A. must surely be involved in some way. Thus, in the late spring of 1965 McGeorge Bundy, the president's national security advisor, asked the FBI to investigate the antiwar movement to determine if there was indeed communist involvement.

Hoover and President Johnson met on April 28, 1965. Johnson expressed extraordinary anxiety over the New Left movement and what it was doing to the country. He told Hoover that, according to intelligence reports reaching him, the North Vietnamese and Red Chinese felt that intensified antiwar agitation in the United States would eventually create a traumatic domestic crisis leading to a complete breakdown in law and order. Thus, according to this line of reasoning, U.S. troops would have to be withdrawn from Vietnam in order to restore domestic tranquility. Quite simply, the president felt that the New Left movement was giving encouragement to the enemies of the United States.

Hoover advised Johnson that the SDS and accompanying groups were planning to demonstrate against the war in eighty-five U.S. cities between May 3 and May 9, 1965—the largest antiwar demonstration to date. The bureau, Hoover said, would prepare "an overall memorandum on the Vietnam demonstrations and communist influence in the same."[4]

The next day, April 29, Hoover issued instructions for a report to be prepared on "what we know about the Students for a Democratic Society." In the memo he stated, "What I want to get to the president is the background with emphasis upon the communist influence therein." He added that the bureau was "to penetrate the Students for a Democratic Society so that we will have proper informant coverage similar to what we have in the Ku Klux Klan and the Communist Party itself."[5]

The final report, titled "Communist Activities Relative to United States Policy on Vietnam" proved that the president and the director were completely off the mark. The report said that CPUSA *wanted* to influence antiwar activity but that their influence on the antiwar movement was quite negligible.

These findings notwithstanding, the White House played an important role in monitoring antiwar activity. By 1966 the bureau was sending undercover informant reports on SDS and related antiwar activist group activities directly to the White House for review on a regular basis.

"Free universities"—attached to a number of major colleges and universities across the nation—came under FBI scrutiny in the spring of 1966. A note of instruction from the bureau advised "that free universities that come to the bureau's attention will be studied to determine if they are in any way related to subversive anti–Vietnam war groups."[6]

Five FBI undercover informants were used to infiltrate the free university at Ann Arbor, Michigan. A ten-page intelligence report was developed on April 15, 1966. It "described in detail the formation, curriculum content and associates of the group—including several members of the Students for a Democratic Society and the Socialist Workers Party."[7] This document was sent to the president, the director, and intelligence agencies throughout the government. Curiously, no further action was taken.

The White House also received name checks from FBI confidential files on dozens of individuals who had signed telegrams "critical of U.S. Vietnam policy."

Antiwar protests and demonstrations continued to escalate all during 1967—in spite of enormously increased surveillance by the FBI, other intelligence agencies, and practically every police force in the country. More than 1 million people demonstrated against the war on April 7, 1967. This largest-ever demonstration was the lead news story on all three major networks. On October 15 the Nationwide Moratorium against the War took place. Again, the sheer weight of numbers expressed the unpopularity of the war: Again, more than 1 million took to the streets all across America.

In late October the antiwar movement struck at the very heart of America's war machinery. More than 35,000 activists mounted a furious charge against troops and marshals defending the Pentagon. To even their surprise, they broke through the line of defenders and, after a bloody melee, briefly occupied a part of the Pentagon itself.

Former FBI Special Agent Wall remembers that the FBI was at the Pentagon demonstration "watching, listening, photographing, and recording the events of the day."[8] Photographers' prints and undercover informant reports obtained on that day were used to create new FBI intelligence files. Individual activists' names were forwarded to headquarters and then on to activists' hometown FBI field offices. Follow-up investigations on almost all individual activists were a matter of procedure. Wall remembers that, "for the 'crime' of expressing dissent against the war in Vietnam, hundreds of citizens became the objects of FBI surveillance and investigation."[9]

Hoover continued to believe that the activists represented a communist attempt to undermine the will of the United States to continue its fight against aggression in Vietnam. With a stunning lack of inquisitiveness, special agents did not question Hoover's view of the world.

A December 1, 1967, memorandum from Hoover to twenty-three selected FBI field offices reflected the bureau's increasing uneasiness with the developing antidraft movement. The memo, almost certainly reflecting immense White House pressure, said that "individual cases are being opened regarding leaders of anti-draft organizations and individuals not connected with such organizations but who are actively engaged in counseling, aiding and abetting the anti-draft movement."[10]

Shortly thereafter, thousands of antiwar, antidraft protestors stormed the military induction center in Oakland, California, during "Stop the Draft Week." Other protestors gathered on Boston Commons and dramatically burned their draft cards. Dow Chemical, a war materials supplier, became a special antiwar target. Dow recruiters were targeted and harassed during "Dow Days" at Harvard as well as the universities of Illinois, Wisconsin, and Minnesota. On November 15, 1967, another million protestors marched against the war.

The year 1967 was, however, a tea party compared to 1968. The vast panorama of American national life was shattered by antiwar violence in almost every U.S. city of consequence. "For what was happening in America in 1968," Theodore White recalled, "had been happening in crescendo for three years before."[11]

Fully 221 major antiwar demonstrations struck 101 colleges and universities during the first six months of 1968, but the occupation and confrontation at Columbia University was the most traumatic to the nation at large. If for no other reason than the fact that the university predated the founding of the American republic itself, Columbia seemed too venerable.

From the FBI director's chair, the most shocking aspect of the Columbia occupation was the timid, lackluster response by university officials. The police were not summoned until several days after the occupation had been completed, and by then the damage was done.

Following the Columbia confrontation, FBI Assistant Director William C. Sullivan received a memo from C. D. Brennan—dated May 9, 1968—that recommended the strongest possible action against antiwar activists. "The New Left," Brennan wrote, "has on many occasions viciously and scurrilously attacked the Director and the Bureau in an attempt to hamper our investigation and to drive us off the college campuses. With this in mind, it is our recommendation that a new Counterintelligence Program be designed to neutralize the New Left and key activists."[12] On that same day, the New Left COINTELPRO was authorized.

A network of undercover informants was already in place within the New Left, and carefully selected wiretaps were ready for further usage.

A May 16, 1968, headquarters memo to COINTELPRO-approved field offices had a tone of urgency: "In view of the increased agitational activity taking place on college campuses, each office is instructed to immediately expand both its coverage and investigation of campus based New Left groups and black nationalist organizations with the objective of determining in advance the plans of these elements to engage in violence or disruptive activities on the campus."[13]

Less than two weeks later, on May 19, violence exploded at Ohio University. Antiwar strikes quickly followed at colleges in Texas, Ohio, and Wisconsin.

The New Left COINTELPRO directives were issued to field offices on May 23. Offices were instructed to gather information on possible false allegations of police brutality in dealing with activists, and to look into the supposed depravity of many New Left adherents. Special agents were to advise college administrators on the value of taking a firm, no-nonsense stand against activists on campus.

Field offices were told that "every avenue of possible embarrassment must be vigorously and enthusiastically explored. It cannot be expected that information of this type will be easily obtained and an imaginative approach by your personnel is imperative to its success."[14]

The bureau had some difficulty defining the term "New Left," which was used in the official name of the new COINTELPRO. Special agents were told that the New Left was a "subversive force" that sought to destroy America's "traditional values." The "New Left" had no "definable ideology"; nevertheless, it had "strong Marxist existentialist, nihilist and anarchist overtones." On another occasion the New Left was described as a "loosely-bound free wheeling, college oriented movement" comprised of "the more extreme and militant anti–Vietnam War and anti-draft protest organizers." The special agent in charge of New Left intelligence later concluded, "It has never been strictly defined, as far as I know. . . . It's more or less an attitude I would think."[15]

The bureau's counterintelligence machinery—already in place against the New Left—began to step up the pace. William C. Sullivan later remembered that "our men in the field had no trouble getting information about the New Left because the majority of students, although they were against the war in Vietnam, were also against the violence that was going on."[16]

On May 29, 1968, a COINTELPRO memo instructed field agents to submit any type of exposé New Left articles to campus newspapers—articles that, the memo said, "should be extremely radical on their face, use profanity or be repulsive in nature." Published articles then would be used for submission to "state legislators and friendly news media, and the like."[17]

An article appeared in the May 20, 1968, issue of *Barron's* entitled "Campus or Battleground? Columbia Is a Warning to All American Universities."[18] The bureau wasted little time in having the article reprinted and mailed anonymously "to college educators who have shown reluctance to take decisive action against the New Left."[19]

A June 7, 1968, COINTELPRO memo from Philadelphia Special Agent William S. Bett demonstrates just how extensive FBI and local law enforcement coverage of the New Left could be on any given occasion. In this situation, the SDS was holding a protest meeting against "research for weapons used in Vietnam." Only 100 activists attended and there were no violent incidents. Nevertheless, there were twenty-two law enforcement personnel monitoring the event. They utilized seven police cars and one communications vehicle. The coordinator of the demonstration was Haverford physics instructor William Davidon. The demonstrators carried placards that read, "Science is for helping people, not removing them in Vietnam or West Philadelphia." There was full television coverage. At the bottom of the memo, Bett noted that the "heavy surveillance paid off in fresh material for the dossiers of ten people and two organizations."[20]

The original New Left letter, as noted, outlined the specifics of the new counterintelligence program. The letter also asked all COINTELPRO-approved field offices to submit suggestions for the new action. The responses were reviewed at headquarters by a team that almost certainly included Hoover, Sullivan, Brennan, Clyde Tolson, and Alan Belmont. The suggestions for COINTELPRO actions against the New Left were used in a July 6, 1968, letter to field offices. These suggestions included the following:

1. preparing leaflets designed to discredit student demonstrators, using photographs of New Left leadership at the respective universities. "Naturally the most obnoxious pictures should be used";

2. instigating "personal conflicts or animosities" between New Left leaders;

3. creating the impression that leaders are "informants for the Bureau or other law enforcement agencies";

4. sending articles from student newspapers of the "underground press"—illustrating the depravity of the New Left—to university officials, donors, legislators, and parents. "Articles showing advocation of the use of narcotics and free sex are ideal";

5. having members arrested on marijuana charges;

6. sending anonymous letters about a student's activities to parents, neighbors, and the parents' employers. "This could have the effect of forcing the parents to take action";

7. sending anonymous letters or leaflets describing the "activities and associations" of New Left faculty members and graduate assistants to university officials, legislators, boards of regents, and the press. "These letters should be signed 'A Concerned Alumni,' or 'A Concerned Taxpayer' "

8. using "cooperative press contacts" to emphasize that the "disruptive elements" constitute a "minority" of the students. "The press should demand an immediate referendum on the issue in question";

9. exploiting the "hostility" among the SDS and other New Left groups toward the SWP, the YSA, and the Progressive Labor party;

10. using "friendly news media" and law enforcement officials to disrupt New Left coffeehouses near military bases—which were attempting to "influence members of the Armed Forces";

11. using cartoons, photographs, and anonymous letters to "ridicule" the New Left; and

12. using "misinformation" to "confuse and disrupt" New Left activities, such as notifying members that events had been canceled.[21]

Twelve COINTELPRO memoranda from the Philadelphia field office to the director—all dated July 8, 1968—detailed the surveillance coverage of New Left operations at Penn State, the University of Pennsylvania, Temple, Lehigh, Bucknell, Franklin and Marshall, Swarthmore, Haverford, Bryn Mawr, and Villanova. These particular memos refer to extensive FBI on-campus observation and, in some cases, disruption of the SDS, the W.E.B. Du Bois clubs, the Philadelphia Anti-draft Union, and the Progressive Labor party.[22]

In light of the fact that 101 colleges had already been hit by violence during the first half of 1968, it is not terribly surprising that bureau memos seem almost obsessive about the potential for even more New Left violence. In most cases, New Left leaders were identified by name. Activities reported by special agents and undercover informants included antidraft counseling, antiwar protests of various types, and extensive picketing of on-campus recruiting efforts by the military, the CIA, and Dow Chemical.

It seems probable that 1968 was Hoover's worst year in office since he became director in 1924. The government's collective intelligence and law-enforcement agencies seemed unable to contain the violence. The president and the director were in constant—perhaps daily—communication. Hoover, as head of the world's largest investigative agency, was in an unenviable position.

On July 23, 1968, Hoover issued a stinging memo to special agents-in-charge. The memo, printed here in part, gives some idea of his frustrations.

> INVESTIGATION OF THE NEW LEFT—There has been a marked increase in recent months of bombings and burnings of public buildings and other acts of terrorism which could logically have been perpetrated by extremist elements of the New Left. New Left leaders have constantly exhorted their followers to abandon their traditional role of "passive dissent" and resort to acts of violence and terrorism as a means of disrupting the defense effort and opposing established authority. Publications of the New Left are replete with articles proposing the bombings of draft boards and other Government installations, and literature containing detailed diagrams and instructions for making incendiary devices has been widely disseminated among New Left groups.
>
> I have been appalled by the reaction of some of our field offices to some of the acts of violence and terrorism which have occurred, such as those which have recently taken place in certain college towns and in some instances on college campuses. While it is recognized that many of these acts do not constitute violations of law within the primary investigative jurisdiction of the Bureau, it is essential, where the strong presumption exists that acts of violence have been perpetrated by New Leftists or other subversive elements under investigation by the Bureau, that every logical effort should be made to resolve through contact with established sources

whether these elements are in fact responsible for such acts. Of course, good judgment and extreme caution must be utilized in this connection so as not to convey the impression to the public or other investigative agencies that we are assuming jurisdiction in those instances where there are not facts which would establish FBI jurisdiction.

It cannot be too strongly emphasized that positive results can be achieved only through the development of adequate high quality informants who are in a position to obtain detailed information regarding the activities and future plans of individuals and organizations affiliated with the New Left movement.

When terroristic acts occur which by reason of the target of the act or by reason of the locale would appear to fit into the objectives of or could have been motivated by subversive elements, particularly New Leftists, I expect an immediate and aggressive response from you in the form of alerting and directing all logical sources and informants into activity to determine if subversive groups could have been responsible.

I have reminded you time and again that the militancy of the New Left is escalating daily. Unless you recognize this and move in a more positive manner to identify subversive elements responsible so that appropriate prosecutive action, whether federally or locally initiated, can be taken, this type of activity can be expected to mount in intensity and to spread to college campuses across the country. This must not be allowed to happen and I am going to hold each Special Agent in Charge personally responsible to insure that the Bureau's responsibilities in this area are completely met and fulfilled.

> Very truly yours,
> John Edgar Hoover
> Director[23]

The most dramatic of the direct confrontations between the New Left and the government took place during the Democratic National Convention in Chicago during the summer of 1968.

The biggest New Left group in Chicago that summer was Dave Dellinger's National Mobilization Committee to End the War in Vietnam (NMC). Dellinger was assisted by Tom Hayden and Rennie Davis. Their forces numbered about 25,000 activists. About forty NMC command posts were used to monitor events and to strike where the most damage could be done.

The security forces marshaled against them were considerable: 11,900

Chicago police, 7,500 Illinois National Guard, 200 Chicago firemen, and 1,000 FBI and Secret Service agents.[24] FBI undercover informants had moved into the crowd in force. Day-by-day intelligence reports at each stage of the action were quickly forwarded to the director in Washington.

Feelings at headquarters, concerning the convention confrontation, ran at a fever pitch. One internal memo excoriated the New Left and castigated the "liberal press and the bleeding hearts and the forces on the left [who] are taking advantage of the situation in Chicago surrounding the Democratic National Convention to attack the police and law enforcement agencies."[25]

An arsenal of COINTELPRO techniques was used in Chicago. In one action, the Chicago field office duplicated the blank housing forms that the National Mobilization Committee to End the War in Vietnam had used when it solicited and obtained housing for demonstrators coming into Chicago. Special agents filled out 217 of these forms with non-existent names and addresses and mailed them to the National Mobilization Committee. The committee then gave them to demonstrators who made "long and useless journeys to locate these addresses."[26] It is not surprising that the committee then decided to discard all replies received on the housing forms.

For the violence it inspired, the Democratic convention has had few equals in American political history. Dave Dellinger later recalled, "The police attacks helped convince millions of people that the society was falling apart and would not return to normal until the war was ended. Thus, we achieved our immediate objective of increasing public disillusionment with the war."[27]

After the smoke cleared, there was almost universal condemnation of the brutality used by the Chicago Police Department. The director brushed the condemnation aside. He still felt that getting tough with students, demonstrators, and administrators would bring the New Left excesses under control.

On August 28, 1968, the director sent additional instructions to the Chicago field office advising the special agent-in-charge to "obtain all possible evidence that would disprove these charges" (that the Chicago police used excessive force), and "to consider measures by which the cooperative news media may be used to counteract these allegations." The memo goes on to say, "When actual evidence of police brutality is not available, it can be expected that these elements will stretch the truth and even manufacture incidents to indict law enforcement agencies. We should be mindful of this situation and develop all possible evidence to expose this activity and to refute these allegations."[28]

In another memo to Chicago, dated September 8, 1968, special agents were told to advise Chicago undercover informants that many incidents were, in fact, *staged* by protestors to bait the police into reacting by force. Further, special agents were to determine if the New Left had violated antiriot statutes. There is nothing in the record to suggest that the bureau was concerned by the fact that the Chicago police *had* used excessive force.[29]

Several more COINTELPRO memos from Hoover followed in quick succession. All advised special agents to "remain alert for and to seek specific data depicting the depraved nature and moral looseness of the New Left" and to "use this material in a vigorous and enthusiastic approach to neutralizing them."[30]

Hoover's next memo appeared several weeks later, on October 28, 1968. The term "New Left," he advised, "does not refer to a definite organization but to a movement which is providing ideologies and platforms alternate to those of existing communist and other basic revolutionary organizations." Also, he asserted that "there is a need to compile a single investigative report—a clear cut picture of the entire New Left movement for the express purpose of assessing its threat to the security of the United States." Additionally, Hoover instructed that quarterly reports on the New Left COINTELPRO were to be submitted and subfiles were to be opened under the following headlines:

Organizations ("when organized, objectives, locality in which active, whether part of a national organization")

Membership (and "sympathizers"—use "best available informants and sources")

Finances (including identity of "angels" and funds from "foreign sources")

Communist Influence

Publications ("describe publications, show circulation and principal members of editorial staff")

Violence

Religion ("support of movement by religious groups or individuals")

Political Activities ("details relating to position taken on political

matters including efforts to influence public opinion, the elec-
torate and Government bodies")

Ideology

Education ("courses given together with any educational outlines
and assigned or suggested reading")

Social Reform ("demonstrations aimed at social reform")

Labor ("all activity in the labor field")

Public Appearances of Leaders ("on radio and television" and "before groups, such as labor, church and minority groups," including "summary of subject matter discussed")

Factionalism

Security Measures

International Relations ("travel in foreign countries," as well as
"attacks on United States foreign policy")

Mass Media ("indications of support of New Left by mass media")[31]

By April 1969 the FBI had more than 2,000 agents investigating the
New Left movement. Additionally, well over 1,000 paid undercover
informants were in operation and reporting their findings to FBI handlers
on a regular basis. In 1969, according to bureau documents, 271 law
enforcement conferences were held by the FBI on the subjects of extremist groups and violence, and more than 23,000 representatives of various criminal-justice and law-enforcement agencies across the United
States attended. The subject of activism, violence, and civil disobedience
was being discussed by everyone at every level of law enforcement. In
the following year, the primary subject was bombing and bomb threats.
More than 33,000 representatives of 8,305 criminal-justice and law-enforcement agencies attended the FBI conferences in 1970.[32]

Until the spring of 1969, the SDS was the most vocal and active of all
the groups in the New Left movement. But that spring, the Weather
Underground broke away from the SDS.

The Weather Underground, which probably numbered no more than
400 members at any time, was the ultraradical, extremely violent wing
of the New Left movement. Their original name, the Weathermen, came
from a verse in Bob Dylan's 1965 song "Subterranean Homesick Blues":
"You don't need a weatherman to know which way the wind blows."[33]

Their rampaging violence horrified much of the nation. Their activities,
as Robert D. McFadden has observed, "estranged even many of the

leftists who shared their liberationist, anti-Establishment views." Many feel—even today—that the Weathermen "besmirched civil rights, anti-war and other legitimate causes and organizations from which they sprang."[34]

On October 8, 1969, the Weather Underground launched their "Days of Rage" rampage in Chicago—an orgy of violence and destruction that hit neighborhoods, business firms, and an army induction center. They followed the Chicago action with nineteen bombings across the country. Targets included the U.S. Capitol building, government facilities in Pittsburgh and New York, and recruiting and draft centers. In an accidental explosion at their bomb factory, in a Greenwich Village townhouse, three people were killed. In 1970 the group disappeared into the underground, and several were not apprehended until the 1980s.

In the meantime, the New Left continued to focus its energies on less violent means of protest. In May 1971 there was an attempt to shut down the government in Washington. Traffic and government buildings were blockaded by human shields of activists, creating nightmarish logistical problems. Thirteen thousand people were arrested. The May 1971 demonstration was, in terms of public recognition, on a par with the Columbia University occupation and the disruption of the Democratic convention.

As was customary, the FBI used a variety of counterintelligence techniques in the New Left COINTELPRO. For example, the use of anonymous mailings directed to or against perceived New Left targets was used throughout this COINTELPRO. On August 27, 1968, the San Antonio field office picked up on an article in the *San Antonio Light*—the student newspaper at the University of Texas at Austin—which was headlined "FREE LOVE COMES TO SURFACE IN AND AROUND UT AUSTIN" and was concerned with the atmosphere of "free love and cohabitation"[35] then said to be in existence at the university. In the bureau's opinion, such a lifestyle was a typical and degrading manifestation of the New Left movement.

After obtaining approval from bureau headquarters, San Antonio worked up a fictitious letter that was supposed to be from a parent who was planning to send his son to the university. This unsigned letter and a copy of the "Free Love" newspaper article were mailed to Texas State Senator Wayne Connally, brother of Governor John Connally, and also to Frank C. Erwig, chairman of the Board of Regents of the University of Texas.

In reference to this COINTELPRO action, a San Antonio memo dated August 27, 1968, noted that "such a communication may be of value in forcing the university to take action against those administrators who are permitting an atmosphere to build up on campus that will be a fertile field for the New Left."[36]

In Newark, the field office learned through an undercover campus informant that members of the student body at Rutgers University were publishing a newspaper called *Screw*. This newspaper, according to bureau documents, contained "a type of filth that could only originate in a depraved mind. . . . The paper is being given away and sold inside Conklin Hall, Rutgers University, Newark by 'hippie' types in unkempt clothes, with wild beards, shoulder-length hair and other examples of their nonconformity."[37] In the bureau's mind, this type of loose and lurid behavior personified the New Left lifestyle. Newark took action.

An anonymous letter was mailed to several members of the Senate Education Committee in the New Jersey State Senate. The letter read, in part, "Would you want your children or grandchildren, especially young girls, subjected to such depravity? . . . [T]his is becoming a way of campus life. Poison the minds of the young, destroy their moral being and in less than one generation this country will be ripe for its downfall. Rutgers is supported by public funds."

The letter was signed by "A Concerned Student."[38]

A New Jersey Senate Education Committee investigation of the matter soon followed.

Elsewhere, in the fall of 1968, the FBI learned that approximately thirty Oberlin College students were engaged in a hunger strike "as a form of protest against the war in Vietnam." Special agents from the Cleveland field office identified two of the students by name. Then, simply by consulting the Oberlin College student directory, the agents determined the students' home addresses. The letter below was sent, anonymously, to the parents of Oberlin College student John Kaza.

Oberlin, Ohio

Dear Mr. and Mrs. Kaza:

I am writing to you in the hope that, as John's parents, you may be able to persuade him of the lack of wisdom in becoming part of a hunger strike by Oberlin students in protest against the Vietnam war. I also oppose this war but I have tried to convince John that fasting to express opposition can only lead to injury to his health and damage to his academic standing. Obviously my efforts have been unsuccessful and I am concerned to the point where I reluctantly am writing this letter to you.

Another part of my concern for John's present conduct is my strong feeling that the hunger strike is being guided and directed by a group of left-wing students who call themselves the Young Socialist Alliance. I don't know too much about this group but I have made some inquiries and everything I have learned thus far indicates they are cynically using John and others for purposes that go far beyond opposition to the war.

I hope you will understand my reasons for writing without divulging my name. I would like to continue as John's friend and I am afraid that, in his present state of emotional involvement, he would not approve of anyone who brought his actions to the attention of his parents. I hope I am doing the right thing.

Sincerely yours,
An interested student[39]

Oberlin College alumnus Eugene Kaza, John Kaza's father, still remembers the anonymous FBI letter after more than twenty years. "The whole Vietnam thing was going on. Students were demonstrating. My son and some others were fasting against the war which was certainly their right. This letter came to our house and we had no idea who it was from. My wife and I were stunned and angry. We really didn't determine that the letter came from the FBI until 1978 or 1979. It seemed like a childish thing for the FBI to do."[40]

An undercover informant in Atlanta advised special agents that Nelson Perry Blackstock, the head of the Atlanta chapter of the Young Socialists Alliance, worked in the mimeograph room at Shell Oil in Atlanta, and was using Shell Oil Company equipment to print literature for the local chapter of the Young Socialists. Some of this literature was distributed during GI Day in Atlanta on October 27, 1968. It was known that another Young Socialists member named Jerry Heard was working in the same department with Blackstock.

After approval from headquarters, the following letter was typed on nonwatermarked paper and mailed in a plain envelope to J. H. Hall, personnel department, Shell Oil Company, Atlanta:

Dear Sirs:

I was riding on a bus the other night and overheard two hippies talking about a peace demonstration. One of these hippies said that they saved a lot of money by using Shell Oil Company printing presses. They talked about some fellow called NELSON who uses Shell Oil Company printing equipment to print propaganda against the war.

I am a Shell Credit Card holder but do not wish to divulge my name; however, I think if this is true that it should be stopped.

Very truly yours,
A Shell customer[41]

The letter must have threaded the needle almost perfectly. J. H. Hall advised a bureau source that Blackstock submitted his resignation on April 18, 1969, and that a review of Blackstock's work record found him "far from satisfactory."[42] A COINTELPRO memorandum to headquarters—dated May 22, 1969—ventured that, in all likelihood, the anonymous bureau letter triggered the review of Blackstock's work record and hence "would have caused his dismissal."[43]

In February 1969, special agents learned that the New Left organization in Atlanta was in some disarray, evidently because of internal disputes among the Socialist Workers party, the Young Socialists Alliance, the SDS, and the Revolutionary Youth Movement. However, by early 1970 it looked as if the groups had put some of their difficulties behind them; they were working together on a major antiwar demonstration designed to coincide with Vice-president Spiro Agnew's planned visit to Atlanta on February 2, 1970. After approval from headquarters, the Atlanta field office prepared an anonymous letter designed to stir up internal tension all over again. The target was David Simpson, a leader in the Revolutionary Youth Movement and coordinator of the forthcoming demonstration. Simpson was warned of the potential Trotskyite domination of the entire Atlanta-area antiwar coalition. It was hoped that the letter would "alienate these groups and frustrate their agitational activity." It read as follows:

Dear Dave,

How can you RYM people be so naive and gullible as to continue to let the Trots run the whole show their way as they did again at the anti-war conference at Emory. It looks like you could see that they have the whole thing figured out, and have all the answers before these so-called "conferences" even start.

As a communist, which they say you are, you sure don't show any knowledge of communist tactics. Why don't you check out your Trot friends on the night before your "conference," and you might find that they are together, busy with plans as to how they will manipulate the coalition to their own specifications—being gracious enough to throw you a few scraps to keep you happy.

Our revolution is a long way off if we have to wait for them to do it their way—they've been carrying the ball for years, now it should be someone else's turn.

A Friend[44]

In New York, the FBI attempted to create disharmony in the local New Left with a letter criticizing the National Steering Committee (NSC) of the New Mobilization Committee to End the War in Vietnam. Purportedly written by one of the committee's own members, the letter took the Steering Committee to task for the organization's racial imbalance and for allegedly allowing Trotskyites to assume far too much influence. Copies were mailed to members of the NMC Steering Committee and to a supporting organization known as the Vietnam Moratorium Committee.

NEW MOBILIZATION COMMITTEE TO END THE WAR
IN VIETNAM
1029 Vermont Avenue, N.W., Washington, D.C. 20005
Area Code 202 737–8600

MEMO TO: National Steering Committee
RE: The Absolute Racial Imbalance of the NSC

Having for a short time served as a member of the NSC, and currently active in the Moratorium Committee—both in Washington and New York, I find it necessary to call attention to certain facts overlooked or shoveled under the rug by NMC leadership.

My understanding at the time I joined NMC was that it was to be run as a non-exclusionary organization—devoted to one primary cause, the immediate end of the frightful war in Vietnam. We were not to be side-tracked into supporting the aims of the militant left. We were not to be sucked into protests against the government's trial of the Conspiracy 8 in Chicago and the like. Our sights were to be adjusted at some later time when the war terminated. Or, so I thought.

Over the past several years the Trotskyites have literally taken control of the body proper and have repeatedly resisted efforts to recruit black brothers into NMC leadership. In addition, they have seen fit to use the good offices of the NMC to further their own political aspirations, nebulous as they are.

I have been sickened—on more than one occasion—by the promises made to the Black United Front, promises not kept, promises made with the mouth and not the heart. The attitude of the Steering Committee towards the BUF was and is a matter of disgrace. In the main, NMC leadership has been no better than the racist politicians and phony liberals who give lip service to the black community and turn their backs on any positive action.

The NMC leadership has demonstrated an appalling lack of sensitivity towards the largest minority in the country. If NMC is to survive the coming months, the situation must be rectified immediately. Our leadership—including the omni-present Trotskyites and other radicals—had better take positive steps before those who disagree with current policy, and there are many, either withhold further support of the _____NMC leadership. It is my belief the NMC would greatly benefit under a leader like Sam Brown of MC [the Moratorium Committee].

To avoid senseless imbroglio, I choose to remain anonymous until the proper time. Just for the record—I am not black.[45]

As noted, the bureau was always concerned about the possible development of a partnership between the Black Panthers and elements of the New Left—particularly the SDS. A number of letters were used to create hostility between the two organizations. The following letter was mailed to local Panther members by the Detroit field office on March 3, 1970.

Dear Brothers and Sisters,

Since when do us Blacks have to swallow the dictates of the honky SDS? Doing this only hinders the Party progress in gaining Black control over Black people. We've been _____over by the white fascists [sic] pigs and the Man's control over our destiny.

We're sick and tired of being severely brutalized, denied our rights and treated like animals by the white pigs. we say to hell with the SDS and its honky intellectual approaches which only perpetuate control of Black people by the honkies.

The Black Panther Party theory for community control is the only answer to our problems and that is to be followed and enforced by all means necessary to insure control by Blacks over all police departments regardless of whether they are run by honkies or uncle toms.

The damn SDS is a paper organization with a severe case of diarrhea of the mouth which has done nothing but feed us lip service. Those few idiots calling themselves weathermen run around like kids on Halloween. A good example is their "militant" activities at the Northland Shopping Center a couple of weeks ago. They call themselves revolutionaries but take a look at who they are. Most of them come from well heeled families even by honky standards. They think they're helping us Blacks but their futile, misguided and above all white efforts only muddy the revolutionary waters.

The time has come for an absolute break with any non-Black group and especially those _____ SDS and a return to our pursuit of a pure black revolution by Blacks for Blacks.

Power!

Off the Pigs!!!![46]

Undercover informants were used constantly during the entire life of the New Left COINTELPRO, primarily to disrupt antiwar plans. Dave Dellinger remembers that SDS and New Mobilization Committee meetings became increasingly secretive and private. Key leaders ultimately refused to discuss antiwar plans openly because it was generally assumed by members that undercover informants were present. In time the bureau's undercover informants were so successful and their penetration was so complete that many of the New Left group leaders all but succumbed to paranoia. Ultimately, any form of democracy within the NMC and the SDS became impossible. As with the KKK infiltration, the FBI could often influence and even direct group policy.

In one case, an informant penetrated an antidraft group that, in addition to protest activities, was also involved with the United Church of Christ in joint welfare projects. This informant, a woman, worked within the group and with the church for a period of eighteen months. She supplied her FBI handlers with more than 1,000 activists' names.

Colleges and universities were, of course, the main focus of special agents working within the New Left COINTELPRO. A memo from the Philadelphia field office, dated September 23, 1970, provides insight into FBI thinking at the time. Written after the shootings at Kent State and much of the violence of the Weather Underground, the memo—from Special Agent William D. Anderson, Jr.—assigned eighteen special agents to monitor antiwar protests at sixty-nine colleges and universities in the greater Philadelphia area. These institutions had a combined enrollment of more than 150,000 students. The memo listed more than seventy categories of protest activity to be monitored. Major headings included such categories as "Student Agitator" or "Students for a Democratic Society." Under the heading "New Left Movement," subcategories included violence, religion, communist influence, student disorder, race relations, publications, mass media, and factionalism.[47] Careful attention was paid to expanding the coverage of campuses by informants. A steady flow of memos stressed that special agents were to exercise extraordinary care in recruiting new student informants.[48]

The technique of "disinformation" was used in many cases, both on and off the campus. For example, an informant working with the Los Angeles field office was instructed to spread a rumor that the leader of a local SDS group was using SDS funds to support a drug habit. The same informant was also instructed to imply in a rumor that a second local SDS leader had stolen SDS funds. The actions created an explosion. The special agent reported that, "as a result of actions taken by this informant, there have been fist fights and acts of name calling at several of the Los Angeles SDS meetings." Following this, members of one Los Angeles SDS faction made early-morning telephone calls to other members and "threatened them and attempted to discourage them from attending SDS meetings."[49]

In commenting on this type of disruptive strategy and other tactics, Frank J. Donner has written that "the New Left COINTELPRO was an undisguised assault by the self-appointed defenders of the American way of life against an entire milieu. The tactics were familiar and had worked well enough in the past: disruption of groups and discrediting of individuals through planted propaganda, anonymous mailings, interviews, snitch jackets, 'disinformation,' notionals, letters to relatives, and the use of right-wing group as enforcers."[50]

In San Diego, the bureau used the COINTELPRO technique of labeling a target as an informant. The target—a man who had been active locally at the radical Message Information Center—had been present, by coincidence, at the arrest of a Selective Service violator. A short time later, again by coincidence, the target witnessed yet another arrest of an antiwar protestor.

This seemed a heaven-sent opportunity for disruption. An undercover informant mentioned at a Message Information Center meeting that it seemed odd that two men had been arrested by federal agents almost immediately after the target learned where they lived. Thus, the San Diego field office could report to headquarters that the target was "completely ostracized by members of the Message Information Center and all of the other individuals throughout the area . . . associated with this and/or related groups."[51]

In Philadelphia, informants within the local SDS chapter were used over an extended period of time to cause disunity. A November 21, 1968, memo to headquarters explained that "one informant precipitated a quarrel between the leader of one of the factions and another active SDS member which resulted in the latter's decision to drop out of the SDS."[52]

In the summer of 1969 the SDS planned to hold a major convention at either Penn State or the University of Pennsylvania. Undercover informants advised officials at both universities that such a conclave would not be in the best interests of either institution. Both schools agreed.

Another Philadelphia memo—this one dated July 23, 1970—advised headquarters that efforts at disruption by area undercover informants were continuing without interruption. More specifically, informants monitored the editorial and business operations of Philadelphia's *Free Press*, a weekly radical paper. They learned that the paper was in deep financial trouble and that officials had misappropriated newspaper funds. Informants passed on this information to the IRS.[53]

In the New Left operation, as in all of the COINTELPROs, the bureau had to walk a fine line between developing productive undercover informants and creating agents provocateurs. As a COINTELPRO memo dated September 16, 1970—previously mentioned in Chapter 1—advised, "While our informants should be privy to everything going on and should rise to the maximum level of their ability in the New Left movement, they should not become the person who carries the gun, throws the bomb, does the robbery or by some specific violative, overt act becomes a deeply involved participant."[54]

New Left informants were often in questionable situations, to say the least. David Sannes, a special agent, served as the undercover liaison between the bureau and extremists in the Seattle area. He later testified that he was instructed by bureau counterintelligence officials to develop a terrorist bombing operation, and to develop the explosives in such a way that they would misfire and kill those who were doing the bombing.

In May 1972, after he left the bureau, Sannes said that he had "decided to make what I have done public so that the people of the United States could be informed of what was going on."[55]

The story of undercover informant Larry D. Grantwohl seems even more sinister. Grantwohl, a Vietnam veteran, was one of the first to penetrate the Weather Underground. He was twenty-five years old in 1970, and quickly became one of the most outspoken and most militant members of the Weather Underground in Cincinnati. The bureau announced repeatedly that they had been unable to penetrate the Underground. But Grantwohl participated in violent demonstrations and bombings while living in Underground collectives in Cincinnati and elsewhere. At the same time he was in regular contact with the FBI and Guy L. Goodwill, the chief Justice Department official in charge of prosecution against the Underground; and Grantwohl supplied information that led to the arrests of various Weathermen.

Grantwohl was known for his skill in handling explosives. As former Weatherman Robert Burlington remembers, "Larry was absolutely a provocateur. I can remember one meeting in Cincinnati where there was a discussion going on about the question of armed political resistance and the various bombings that had occurred. Grantwohl took the initiative as was his wont and began castigating people for talking about the destruction of property; he said it wasn't enough to carry on these kinds of bombings. 'True revolutionaries,' he said, 'had to be ready and anxious to kill people.' "[56]

As an informant, Grantwohl was by definition in a very precarious position between law enforcement and the Underground. Under these extremely difficult circumstances, he was able to supply the bureau with precious information about the Underground.

Much of the bureau's effort against the New Left involved the "friendly media," who aided the FBI in "placing unfavorable articles and documentaries about targeted groups, and leaking derogatory information intended to discredit individuals."[57] These operations were generally handled by the FBI Crimes Records Division.

In 1969 the bureau used a friendly media connection, the *Chicago Tribune*, to help disrupt the SDS national convention. Special agents supplied information to *Tribune* reporter Ron Koziol regarding the internal struggle for control of the SDS. On June 17, 1969, the paper ran a front-page story headlined "RED UNIT SEEKS SDS RULE."[58] On June 30, Chicago special agent-in-charge M. S. Johnson advised headquarters

that the article "aggravated a tense situation and helped create the confrontation that split the SDS."[59]

The Philadelphia field office proved to be particularly skillful in the
use of friendly media. In the fall of 1968, the *Philadelphia Inquirer* featured
an article that was headlined, "TO END ANARCHY ON THE CAMPUS"
and was based on J. Edgar Hoover's message published in the September
1968 *Law Enforcement Bulletin*. A Philadelphia memo to the director, dated
September 6, 1968, suggested that "the Bureau may desire to direct a
letter to him [the paper's editor] of approval or appreciation concerning
this editorial."[60]

The bureau worked with the *Philadelphia Bulletin* in the summer of
1970 to produce a series of lengthy articles on "the new revolutionaries."
The first installment explained to the public what the bureau could and
could not do in countering the New Left. Another discussed in considerable detail the New Left fugitives that the FBI was then pursuing.
Court cases that authorized the bureau's antiradical campaign were
cited.

College institutions continued to be COINTELPRO targets.

In one situation, the Pittsburgh field office targeted a university professor who had publicly surrendered his draft card. The same individual
had also been arrested for his part in several antidraft demonstrations.
Special agents contracted a foundation known to be a major benefactor
of the university where the instructor taught and suggested "that the
[foundation] may desire to call to the attention of the University administration questions concerning the advisability of [the professor's] continuing his position there."[61]

The Detroit office also attempted to discredit a university professor
who protested U.S. policy in Vietnam. In this instance, the field office
sent an anonymous letter to political figures, the media, college administrators, and the university's board of regents—flatly accusing the professor of "giving aid and comfort to the enemy."[62]

Two university professors were targeted by the Mobile, Alabama, field
office in late 1970. These two professors were involved in support of an
underground newspaper that was described as "left of center." Special
agents believed that, if the professors were forced to withdraw their
support, the newspaper would quickly fail and the local voice of the
New Left would be silenced. An anonymous letter was sent to the
university administration warning that the instructors' support of the
left-of-center newspaper would be made public if they did not halt their

activities. Both professors were placed on probation by the university president in early 1971.

In a variation of the anonymous mailings, the FBI occasionally produced its own anti–New Left pamphlets and newsletters. The Indianapolis field office requested permission to produce its own newsletter to be distributed on the campus of Indiana University. As in all cases, headquarters cautioned the Indianapolis office against embarrassing the bureau in any way. The newsletter was named the *Armageddon News*. Its sole purpose was to disrupt the New Left at Indiana University.

Vol. 1, #1   9/27/68

PURPOSE

ARMAGEDDON NEWS will be prepared and distributed periodically by a group of concerned IU students who have returned to our school campus this fall to expose at Indiana University the
"CONSPIRACY OF THE NEW LEFT"
We feel the majority at IU abhor the devious and disgusting actions last year of the New Left Hippie Breed. We have spent considerable time and effort to get the straight *"dope"* on these pseudostudents, and we intend to keep you *WELL INFORMED*.

LAST YEAR

In this first issue, we want to highlight last year's activities.

Some will recall that IU had the distinction of being named as organizing Indiana for the March on Washington, D.C. in October, 1967. Mark Ritchey led his dissidents to our capitol where the press reported obscene behavior rarely connected in the past with IU's academic traditions. Encouraged by this support, the Committee to End the War in Vietnam, led by Mark Ritchey and Russell Block, and the Students for a Democratic Society, led by Dan Kaplan and Robin Hunter, and their ilk, stormed the police guard and took over a room of the Business Building where Dow Chemical was interviewing applicants. . . .
. . . SHADES OF COLUMBIA!
Thirty-five hippie leftists were arrested and all convicted.

Not to be dismayed, the very next day, the last day of October, they gave IU its darkest hour with the ill-mannered and obnoxious behavior in "receiving" Secretary of State Dean Rusk at IU Convocation. They, who demand freedom of speech, refused to allow him to present his views. About 300 hissed, booed, and screamed names, and it was very enlightening that many thousands of IU students signed an apology to the Secretary.

In the second semester, Robert Grove and Larry Waxberg, his loyal lieutenant, did not reorganize the DuBois Club. David Colton, a math instructor who went to Canada, insinuated they had formed a Communist Party club at IU to replace it this fall—*WATCH FOR IT!!!!* Grove was able to get James West and Ted Pearson, members of the National Committee of the Communist Party, USA, to come to IU at the end of the semester to help recruit members.

NEXT ISSUE

We have been able to infiltrate members into the *New Left* organizations at IU. We intend to expose officers, members and activities of *all* New Left organizations at IU. Watch for the next issues for details of the:

  Students for a Democratic Society
  Committee to End the War in Vietnam
  W.E.B. DuBois Club
  Communist Party
  Young Socialist Alliance

"DON'T LET THE NEW LEFT WIN THE ARMAGEDDON AT I.U."

The *Armageddon News* was mailed a number of times to selected students on the campus. A memo to headquarters, dated December 17, 1968, claimed that "this distribution was greatly responsible in limiting the number of curious students which normally follow such organizations during this period."[63]

The FBI also used electronic surveillance to infiltrate the New Left.

Targets included a "New Left activist" and an underground publication known in the bureau records as "Publication of Clandestine Underground Group Dedicated to Student Sabotage," as well as the New Mobilization Committee and the Vietnam Moratorium Committee.

In a June 16, 1970, memo to the attorney general, Hoover advised that wiretaps had "obtained information concerning the activities of the national headquarters of [the group and] plans for [the group's] support and participation in demonstrations supporting antiwar groups and the [excised]." It was also noted that the wiretap "revealed . . . contacts with Canadian student elements."[64] (The excised words have been deleted by the FBI.)

The New Left COINTELPRO, along with the other COINTELPROs, ceased operations on April 28, 1971. In total, the FBI had received 381 proposals from approved field offices. Of this total, 285 actions were implemented, with known results obtained in seventy-seven actions. Anonymous or fictitious mailings were used in 40 percent of the New Left actions. In twenty-five cases, special agents disseminated public-record information to media sources. Employers and credit bureaus were informed of New Left member status in twenty situations. In eight cases, the bureau contacted businesses and individuals who had economic dealings with New Left members, and informed them of the members' political affiliations. In twelve actions, the bureau contacted family members and friends of New Left activists.

Without the Vietnam War, there almost certainly would have been no New Left movement. The war was a catastrophe of almost inconceivable dimensions—over 58,000 dead with more than 300,000 casualties. It is difficult to determine whether American participation in the Vietnam War would have ended when it did if there had been no antiwar movement.

No matter how much one may disapprove of the movement's morality or methods, it is certain that those who protested the war were acting within the unmistakable guarantees of the Constitution. In the New Left COINTELPRO, as in the others, the FBI clearly violated those guarantees on many occasions.

NOTES

1. Theodore H. White, *The Making of the President 1968* (New York: Atheneum Publishers, 1969), p. 190.

2. William C. Sullivan with Bill Brown, *The Bureau: My Thirty Years in Hoover's FBI* (New York: W. W. Norton, 1979), p. 148.

3. White, *Making of the President 1968*, p. 215.

4. Senate Select Committee to Study Governmental Operations with Respect to Intelligence Activities, Book III, 94th Cong., 2d sess., 14 Apr. 1976, p. 484.

5. Ibid., pp. 484, 485.

6. FBI Memorandum, Headquarters to Detroit Field Office, 17 Feb. 1966.

7. FBI Memorandum, Detroit Field Office to Headquarters, 15 Apr. 1966.

8. Paul Cowan, Nick Egleson, and Nat Hentoff, *State Secrets: Police Surveillance in America* (New York: Holt, Rinehart & Winston, 1974), p. 254.

9. Ibid., p. 255.

10. FBI Memorandum, Headquarters to Field Office, 1 Dec. 1967.

11. White, *Making of the President 1968*, p. 190.

12. FBI Memorandum, C. D. Brennan to W. C. Sullivan, 9 May 1968.

13. FBI Memorandum, Headquarters to Field Offices, 16 May 1968.

14. FBI Memorandum, Headquarters to Field Offices, 23 May 1968.

15. Senate Committee to Study Government Operations with Respect to Intelligence Activities, "FBI Intelligence Deposition, 28 Oct. 1975," Book III, 94th Cong., 2d sess., 14 Apr. 1976, pp. 22–27.

16. Sullivan with Brown, *Hoover's FBI*, p. 151.

17. FBI Memorandum, Headquarters to Field Offices, 27 May 1968.

18. Robert Hessen, "Campus or Battleground? Columbia Is a Warning to All American Universities," *Barron's*, 20 May 1968.

19. FBI Memorandum, Philadelphia Field Office to Headquarters, 23 Aug. 1968; ibid., 3 Oct. 1968; FBI Memorandum, Headquarters to Philadelphia Field Office, 30 Aug. 1968.

20. FBI Memorandum, Philadelphia Field Office to Headquarters, 7 June 1968.

21. FBI Memorandum, Headquarters to Field Offices, 6 July 1968.

22. FBI Memorandum, Philadelphia Field Office to Headquarters, 8 July 1968.

23. FBI Memorandum, Headquarters to Field Offices, 23 July 1968.

24. White, *The Making of the President 1968*, p. 261.

25. FBI Memorandum, Headquarters to Chicago Field Office, 28 Aug. 1968.

26. FBI Memorandum, Chicago Field Office to Headquarters, 6 Sept. 1968; FBI Memorandum, C. D. Brennan to W. C. Sullivan, 15 Aug. 1968.

27. Dave Dellinger, *More Power than We Know* (Garden City, N.Y.: Anchor Press, 1975), p. 125.

28. FBI Memorandum, Headquarters to Chicago Field Office, 28 Aug. 1968.

29. FBI Memorandum, Headquarters to Chicago Field Office, 8 Sept. 1968.

30. FBI Memorandum, Headquarters to Field Offices, 9 Oct. 1968.

31. FBI Memorandum, Headquarters to Field Offices, 28 Oct. 1968.

32. FBI Memorandum, Headquarters to Field Offices, 15 Aug. 1974.

33. Lucinda Franks, "U.S. Inquiry Finds 37 in Weather Underground," *New York Times*, 5 Mar. 1975, p. 38.

34. Robert D. McFadden, "Issue of Conspiracy: As Investigators Seek Terrorist Links, Scope of Radical Threat Is Debated," *New York Times*, 26 Oct. 1981, pp. 8–9.

35. "Free Love Comes to Surface in and around UT Austin," *San Antonio Light*, 11 Aug. 1968, p. 14B.

36. FBI Memorandum, San Antonio Field Office to Headquarters, 27 Aug. 1968.

37. FBI Memorandum, Newark Field Office to FBI Headquarters, 23 May 1969.

38. FBI Memorandum, FBI Headquarters to Newark Field Office, 4 June 1969.

39. FBI Memorandum, Cleveland Field Office to Headquarters, 25 Nov. 1968.

40. Eugene Kaza, telephone interview with author, 23 Oct. 1989; John Kaza, telephone interview with author, 4 Aug. 1990.

41. FBI Memorandum, Atlanta Field Office to Headquarters, 11 Feb. 1969; FBI Memorandum, Headquarters to Atlanta Field Office, 20 Feb. 1969.

42. FBI Memorandum, Atlanta Field Office to Headquarters, 22 May 1969.

43. Ibid.

44. FBI Memorandum, Atlanta Field Office to Headquarters, 21 Jan. 1970; FBI Memorandum, Headquarters to Atlanta Field Office, 6 Feb. 1970.

45. FBI Memorandum, New York Field Office to Headquarters, 3 Feb. 1970; ibid., 20 Jan. 1970.

46. FBI Memorandum, Detroit Field Office to FBI Headquarters, 10 Feb. 1970; FBI Memorandum, FBI Headquarters to Detroit Field Office, 3 Mar. 1970.

47. Cowan, Egleson, and Hentoff, *State Secrets*, p. 144.

48. Senate Select Committee to Study Governmental Operations with Respect to Intelligence Activities, "The Use of Informants in FBI Domestic Intelligence Investigations," Book III, 94th Cong., 2d sess., 14 Apr. 1976, pp. 227–44.

49. FBI Memorandum, Los Angeles Field Office to Headquarters, 12 Dec. 1968.

50. Frank J. Donner, *The Age of Surveillance* (New York: Alfred A. Knopf, 1980), p. 232.

51. FBI Memorandum, San Diego Field Office to Headquarters, 17 Feb. 1969; FBI Memorandum, Headquarters to San Diego Field Office, 3 Mar. 1969; FBI Memorandum, San Diego Field Office to Headquarters, 30 Apr. 1969.

52. FBI Memorandum, Headquarters to Philadelphia Field Office, 23 July 1970.

53. Ibid.

54. FBI Memorandum, "The New Left Notes—Philadelphia," Philadelphia Special Agent-in-charge, 9 Sept. 1970; FBI Memorandum, "COINTELPRO–New Left," Headquarters to Field Offices, 16 Sept. 1970.

55. Dellinger, *More Power*, p. 78.

56. Seymour M. Hersh, "FBI Informer Is Linked to Bombing and Protest by Weatherman Group," *New York Times*, 20 May 1973, p. 52.

57. Senate Select Committee to Study Governmental Operations with Respect to Intelligence Investigations, "COINTELPRO: The FBI's Covert Action Programs against American Citizens," Book III, 94th Cong., 2nd Sess., 14 Apr. 1976, p. 35.

58. Donner, *Age of Surveillance*, p. 233.

59. FBI Memorandum, Chicago Field Office to Headquarters, 30 June 1969.

60. FBI Memorandum, Philadelphia Field Office to Headquarters, 6 Sept. 1968.

61. FBI Memorandum, Headquarters to Pittsburgh Field Office, 1 May 1970.

62. FBI Memorandum, Detroit Field Office to Headquarters, 11 Oct. 1966; FBI Memorandum, Headquarters to Detroit Field Office, 26 Oct. 1969.

63. FBI Memorandum, Indianapolis Field Office to Headquarters, 17 Dec. 1968.

64. FBI Memorandum, Headquarters to the Attorney General, 16 June 1970.

7 The End of COINTELPRO?

As you know, my committee is interested in looking into the COINTELPRO operations.

Senator Sam J. Ervin, Jr.
Chairman, Subcommittee on
Constitutional Rights

In 1972, NBC newsman Carl Stern was responsible for coverage of the Senate Judiciary Committee in Washington, D.C. In this capacity he contacted committee staff members almost every day; he knew many personally.

During a routine visit to committee headquarters in January 1972, Stern noticed a document on a staff member's desk that was entitled "COINTELPRO–New Left." "What does 'COINTELPRO–New Left' mean?" he asked some staff members.

The staffers didn't know. Stern remembers that "they were as interested in knowing the answers as I was. They could see from the documents themselves that FBI agents had gone beyond their normal investigative functions, but had no idea that COINTELPRO was as extensive or elaborate as it turned out to be."[1] Stern next made several

calls to contacts within the Justice Department about COINTELPRO–
New Left. His calls were not returned.

On March 20, 1972, the newsman wrote to Richard Kleindienst, then
deputy attorney general, and requested information on COINTELPRO–
New Left.

March 20, 1972

Honorable Richard Kleindienst
Deputy Attorney General
United States Department of Justice
Washington, D.C. 20530

Dear General Kleindienst,

Please consider this a Freedom of Information Act request for
access to the following documents:

1) Whatever letter authorized the Federal Bureau of Investigation to establish and maintain its counter-intelligence program de-
nominated "COINTELPRO–New Left."

2) Whatever letter, if any, terminated such program.

3) Whatever letters, if any, ordered or authorized any changes
in the purpose, scope or nature of the program.

I have previously requested such information from the Justice
Department's Public Information Office and from Thomas Bishop,
Assistant Director of the Bureau. In both cases I was given a cour-
teous but clear refusal.

As a lawyer who occasionally lectures on the Freedom of Information Act, I believe I am entitled to the above information. I have
also consulted with Congressman Moorhead's Government Information Subcommittee, the University of Missouri's Freedom of
Information Act Center here, and the American Civil Liberties
Union, all of whom concurred in my judgment.

I thank you for whatever help you can provide in expediting my
request.

Cordially,
Carl Stern
NBC News–Washington[2]

Stern's request was made under the provisions of the Freedom of
Information Act (Title 5, U.S. Code, Sec. 552). His request was refused.
The refusal was based on certain exemptions in the act as interpreted

by the Department of Justice: confidential files of an FBI agent, unofficial defense data, and confidential interagency correspondence.

On June 30, Stern wrote to the new deputy attorney general, Ralph E. Erickson, renewing his request for information. This second request was denied on August 21, 1972.[3]

Sometime in late July, Stern had lunch with L. Patrick Gray III, then the acting director of the FBI. As a follow-up, Stern again requested information on COINTELPRO–New Left in a letter dated September 6, 1972.[4] His request for information was again denied. Stern decided to take the matter to court.

In early 1973 he filed suit in the U.S. District Court for the District of Columbia, appealing the Justice Department's rulings. Stern sought two documents. The first was a letter dated May 10, 1968, addressed to a field official from FBI headquarters in Washington, officially authorizing the "COINTELPRO–New Left" action. The second—a communication from headquarters to all field offices—cancelled all existing COINTEL-PRO operations as of April 28, 1971.

On July 16, 1973, the FBI delivered, in response to the district court's request, copies of the two documents in question to U.S. District Judge Barrington D. Parker. After reviewing them, the judge decided that the documents should be given to Stern; and on December 6, 1973, the requested COINTELPRO documents were given to the NBC reporter.

On the day before the documents were turned over, Clarence M. Kelley—then director of the FBI—had issued a special precautionary memo to all special agents-in-charge nationwide. He mentioned the anticipated publicity surrounding the developing COINTELPRO disclosures and how they might elicit concern over possible violation of individual liberties. FBI employees, he emphasized, were to refrain from engaging in investigative activity that could abridge in any way the rights guaranteed by the Constitution. Neither were they to conduct themselves in any way that might result in defaming the character, reputation, integrity, or dignity of any citizen or organization.[5]

Two days later, Kelley authorized a national press release on the COINTELPRO operations and the social upheavals that had made them necessary. Kelley stressed that at times of national crisis the government would have been derelict in its duty had it not taken every legal measure to protect the fabric of society. The FBI had, Kelley said, the responsibility of investigating allegations of criminal violations and of gathering intelligence regarding threats to the nation.[6]

That same day, December 7, Kelley received from Carl Stern a personal letter in which Stern requested additional COINTELPRO documents, including the following:

> Whatever documents authorized and defined the programs COIN-TELPRO–Espionage; COINTELPRO–Disruption of White Hate Groups; COINTELPRO–Communist Party, U.S.A.; Counter-intelligence and Special Operations; COINTELPRO–Black Extremists; Socialist Workers Party–Disruption Program. Whatever documents directed changes in the programs. Whatever documents authorized a counterintelligence action of any kind after 4/28/71.[7]

Also on that day, reporter Fred Graham of CBS News requested access to documents relating to COINTELPRO–New Left, and to all documents relating to any other COINTELPRO programs.

Director Kelley answered Carl Stern's letter on December 26, 1973, informing him that the documents he requested were in the bureau's confidential investigatory files for law enforcement purposes. Therefore, they were exempt from public disclosure according to the provisions of Title 5, U.S. Code, Section 552(b)(7). Stern could, Kelley said, appeal his decision through judicial review or by writing directly to the attorney general.[8]

Stern chose the latter option. Attorney General William B. Saxbe agreed on March 6, 1974, to supply "part, but not all," of the requested materials.

Stern received a document from the FBI COINTELPRO files dealing with white hate groups, two documents on black extremists, one regarding the Socialist Workers party, and three memoranda under the general classification "Counterintelligence and Special Operations." Individual names and places were deleted from the released materials, and a number of classified secret papers were not released. One day later, seven additional COINTELPRO documents were given to Carl Stern under the Freedom of Information Act. The following day Fred Graham was given the same material.

In the meantime, Saxbe had advised Kelley by letter that President Ford was requesting information about FBI counterintelligence programs. Saxbe had therefore asked Assistant Attorney General Henry Petersen to create an interdepartmental committee to review all FBI files, documents, and papers relating to COINTELPRO operations. The committee was comprised of four attorneys from the Criminal Division of the Department of Justice and three representatives from the Federal Bureau of Investigation selected by Kelley. The director chose Inspector Thomas Smith and Special Agents James Williamson and Edward Pistey.

The committee was at work before the end of January 1974. The members reviewed document summaries compiled directly from the FBI COINTELPRO control files. The identities and affiliations of the various COINTELPRO targets were deleted from the study.

About the time the Petersen Committee was beginning its work, Kelley received a lengthy inquiry from Senator Sam J. Ervin, Jr., chairman of the Subcommittee on Constitutional Rights, Senate Committee on the Judiciary.

Senator Ervin's letter read, "This subcommittee will conduct an inquiry into FBI domestic surveillance activities and [would need] detailed information on the so-called COINTELPRO operations." His letter contained almost eighty specific questions.[9]

Immediately after the letter arrived, Kelley got a direct call from Senator Ervin. "Mr. Kelley, I wanted to follow up my letter of the eighth. As you know, my committee is interested in looking into the COINTELPRO operations," the senator said.

"Thank you for calling, Senator," Kelley replied. "I have your letter in front of me right now."

"We need your assistance, sir. I hope my request for information won't place too great a burden on the FBI," Ervin said.

"I will study your letter, Senator, and prepare my reply by this afternoon. Will that be acceptable?"

"That will be helpful, very helpful. We just want to understand, Mr. Kelley, the policy reasons for developing those programs in the first place, how they operated, and some other matters."

"As you know, Senator, these programs are already under review by the Justice Department," Kelley said.

"I understand that, Mr. Kelley, and I assume that we will receive a copy of their final report. However, my subcommittee wanted to look into the matter also, perhaps in greater detail. I'm sure you understand."

"A discussion of this sort, the discussion of sensitive intelligence issues in an open forum is frankly of concern to me, Senator," Kelley replied.

"I understand your concern, Mr. Kelley, and I share it. But my subcommittee must know more about this. Anything you can do to help us will certainly be appreciated. Please get back to me as soon as possible."[10]

In Kelley's written response, he told the senator that the FBI was unable to comply with the subcommittee's request. Kelley felt there were compelling reasons why the COINTELPRO operations should not be discussed in a public forum. He stressed that the confidentiality of original investigative data as well as the bureau's network of informants must be protected. Classified secret information was implicitly exempt from disclosure under the Freedom of Information Act, Kelley reminded Ervin. The public disclosure of the specific techniques and operations used to counter any subversive intelligence activity in the United States could cause catastrophic damage to the future effectiveness of FBI countersubversion efforts; exposing the identities of FBI private sources and double agents would actually jeopardize their lives.

Kelley suggested that the COINTELPROs could be reviewed in executive session of the Senate oversight subcommittee on the FBI. After consideration, Senator Ervin agreed to the director's suggestion.

On May 24, 1974, Assistant Attorney General Petersen's report on the COINTELPROs was completed.[11] At the time that the report was finished, the director as well as other officials within the government believed that it should remain confidential.

History has shown that the Petersen Report was quite superficial and not nearly so critical as it should have been. The report went only as far as saying that members of organizations targeted by COINTELPRO *might*, in some instances, have been deprived of their rights under the First Amendment to the Constitution.

The committee took into account two basic factors. First, many COINTELPROs were developed in response to public demand that the FBI contain and neutralize the radical forces of social upheaval in the 1960s. (This was true of the White Hate Group COINTELPRO, the Black Nationalist Hate Group COINTELPRO, and the New Left COINTELPRO; there had been no public demand for the Communist Party U.S.A. and Socialist Workers party programs.) Second, each program had been approved in advance by J. Edgar Hoover.

In June 1974, Attorney General Saxbe and FBI Director Kelley briefed the FBI oversight subcommittee (a subcommittee of the Senate Judiciary Committee) on many aspects of the COINTELPROs. In accordance with Kelley's agreement with Senator Ervin, it was held in a closed executive session. About the same time, the comptroller general of the United

States asked for COINTELPRO data—as did Peter Rodino, the chairman of the House Judiciary Committee. Specifically, Congressman Rodino asked that the House Subcommittee on Civil Rights be briefed on the COINTELPRO operations.

On June 20, Saxbe and Kelley attended the graduation of the ninety-seventh class of the FBI Academy at Quantico, Virginia. Saxbe was the commencement speaker. In his speech he referred to the COINTELPRO programs. He said that it was his personal conviction that the Federal Bureau of Investigation set up these programs in the first place because of deep concern for the security of the United States. However, he did go on to say that problems arise when intelligence-gathering techniques cross over into the questionable arena of disruption tactics.

"The dirty tricks are over," Saxbe said. "Law enforcement at every level must operate within the letter of the law."[12]

As noted, Kelley (along with several members of the Petersen Committee) believed that the final report was not to be released to the public. In October the FBI director learned that Saxbe had decided he should release the findings of the Petersen Report to the press.

Kelley immediately called a meeting with his seventeen highest assistants—the executive committee, the top management of the FBI. They discussed their position and possible courses of action in light of the imminent disclosure of more COINTELPRO documents.

The FBI management team unanimously felt that there should be no additional release of COINTELPRO documents and papers under the Freedom of Information Act. Those materials were unquestionably investigatory data and, as a result, exempt from release. The FBI would deny future requests for COINTELPRO documents and let the courts decide the issue. Judicial review would determine whether the documents were indeed privileged by virtue of their investigatory nature. The bureau believed that the courts would rule in their favor. If not, they would cooperate with the courts.

Four days later a COINTELPRO meeting was held in the office of Congressman Rodino. It was attended by Kelley, Saxbe (who called the meeting), Peter Rodino, Edward Hutchinson (the ranking minority member of the House Judiciary Committee), and several other government officials.

The meeting was not stormy, but strong feelings were emphatically expressed. To begin, Saxbe read aloud the entire Petersen Report and

then voiced his own opinion about disclosure: "The COINTELPRO matter has been discussed at some length with the Senate's FBI oversight
committee. I've also reviewed the departmental analysis of COINTEL-
PRO with the committee. I've discussed COINTELPRO and the analysis
with Senator Ervin privately. He is a strong proponent of Freedom of
Information but opposes the release of the COINTELPRO report."

One of the congressmen asked, "How do the rest of the Senate committee members feel about releasing the COINTELPRO report to the
public?"

"They are all opposed to the release of the report; they also oppose
the appointment of a special prosecutor to investigate the matter," Saxbe
replied.

"What is your position, Mr. Saxbe?" Rodino asked.

"I really don't see how we can avoid releasing the report to the public.
First of all, we have the matter of the college professor at Arizona State
who was fired from his job because of an anonymous letter sent by the
FBI. The professor has filed suit and has probably been given some back
pay, and he has requested, under Freedom of Information, the FBI
background file on him. I don't see how we can turn him down."

The attorney general expressed his opinion that the FBI had "gone
beyond the letter of the law" in its COINTELPRO programs and, as far
as he could determine, "no attorney general had been aware of the
programs when they were in operation."

Kelley then addressed the group. He pointed out that "Mr. Saxbe has
gotten his historical facts wrong. Attorneys general going back to the
first Eisenhower Administration were aware of—and approved—the
basic COINTELPRO activities," he said. "In fact, presidential directives
for aggressive counterintelligence programs similar to COINTELPRO
actually date back to the Roosevelt presidency at the opening of the
Second World War," he added.

He mentioned the important National Security Council meeting held
on March 8, 1956, when J. Edgar Hoover proposed a number of very
specific COINTELPRO methodologies to a group that included not only
Attorney General Herbert Brownell but also President Eisenhower.

"The most critical issue of all," he suggested, "was not who knew
and approved of COINTELPRO practices, but what harm a full public
disclosure would do at this time. Full disclosure would doubtless affect
the overall operation of the FBI. Not only would it undermine our credibility with the American people, but such disclosure might well result
in an inability to develop and use informants.

"Speaking of informants," Kelley added, "a number of good, innocent citizens who had been associated with COINTELPROs in the past would now suffer undue hardships—if their involvement were to become public knowledge." Kelley paused to let his audience—especially Saxbe—ponder that.

"Those involved in COINTELPRO activities did what they believed to be in the best interest of the country at that time, and to try to defend COINTELPRO operations of the past in today's world will probably make matters worse," Kelley said. He concluded by repeating that the matters under discussion were in FBI investigative files and thereby excluded from disclosure under the Freedom of Information Act.

Saxbe countered by arguing that various communications about COINTELPRO actions were not purely investigative—and were therefore subject to release. "And I'd like to point out that President Ford favors disclosure, and that certain members of the press already know of at least a portion of COINTELPRO," Saxbe said. "Besides, it will be only a matter of time before the whole COINTELPRO story is revealed."[13]

On November 18, 1974, Saxbe held his long-awaited press conference. He released a summary of the Petersen Report, which had been sharply edited to remove sensitive information. In a very moderate statement that accompanied the release, Saxbe said that there were seven basic COINTELPROs—five domestic programs and two foreign. The COINTELPRO operations had been ongoing between 1956 and 1971. During that time, 3,257 counterintelligence proposals had been made to FBI leaders. Of those, 2,370 had been implemented. In less than 500 of these were the results quantifiable.[14] The great majority of the cases utilized practices and techniques that were legitimate. In only 1 percent of all COINTELPRO activities and techniques could it be argued that the FBI had acted improperly or illegally, Saxbe pointed out. Nevertheless, he felt that certain tactics "must be considered to be abhorrent in a free society such as ours." All the programs had now been canceled, he stated in conclusion.[15]

But as we have seen, there were many outrageous constitutional violations against a number of COINTELPRO targets. In late 1974, when Saxbe made these statements, a complete analysis of all the COINTELPRO operations had not been finished.

Director Clarence M. Kelley, an FBI special agent for twenty-one years, had to defend the COINTELPRO actions of the bureau although he privately disagreed with many of the methods.

Kelley issued a news release on November 18, 1974. "The FBI's intent," he noted, "was to prevent dangerous acts against individuals, organizations, and institutions—public and private—across the United States. FBI employees in these programs had acted in good faith and within the bounds of what was expected of them by the president, the attorney general, Congress, and, I believe, a majority of the American people."

He reminded those who now criticized the FBI that the U.S. Capitol building had been bombed, and that explosions had rocked countless other buildings in American cities. Rioters led by revolutionary extremists had laid siege to military, industrial, and educational facilities. Radical violence had sent shock waves from Maine to California.

Kelley gave specific examples: a bombing at the University of Wisconsin; Chicago's "four days of rage"; racial riots in virtually every city; the murders of Robert F. Kennedy and Martin Luther King, Jr.; the horror outside the Democratic convention site in Chicago in 1968; the antiwar violence on campuses. In most cases, the victims of these illegal acts were citizens who looked to the FBI and other law enforcement agencies to protect *their* lives, *their* property, and *their* civil rights.[16]

On November 20, two days after the Saxbe press conference, Deputy Attorney General Lawrence Silberman, Assistant Attorney General Henry Petersen, and Clarence Kelley testified before the Subcommittee on Civil Rights and Constitutional Rights of the House Judiciary Committee.

Kelley assured the subcommittee that the COINTELPRO programs had been discontinued, but again defended those in the FBI who implemented and conducted the programs. "Should questions arise in the future about similar programs," he said, "I would consult with the attorney general before implementation."[17]

Many of the questions from the House subcommittee were quite incisive. Others—obviously designed to score points with the public—were acrimonious. Exchanges were often sharp. In the end, the FBI and Justice Department officials did agree on the need for a joint congressional committee of oversight to monitor domestic counterintelligence activities.

In the same month, November 1974, Attorney General Saxbe requested that Assistant Attorney General Stanley Pottinger of the Justice

Department's Civil Rights Division conduct a review of COINTELPRO activities to determine if, in fact, civil rights violations had occurred.

On December 1, 1974, William C. Sullivan—one of the original creators of the COINTELPRO operations—said that the FBI should be relieved of authority over domestic intelligence programs. In an interview with the *New York Times*, Sullivan declared, "As [the agency] is now structured it is a potential threat to our civil liberties and should have its power and funds reduced." In sharply criticizing the bureau's past performance in domestic intelligence, Sullivan proposed the development of a new independent board to choose future FBI directors and also to review requests for domestic surveillance.

Sullivan's criticism, coming at a time when the bureau was already receiving a great deal of flak, stunned those within the bureau who had worked with him on the COINTELPRO operations. Sullivan went on to say that it was ludicrous for the American people to picture the FBI "as an elite corps, far superior to any other governmental organization, Federal, State or local. The gulf between public relations and our actual performances was very great indeed."[18]

On January 3, 1975, Assistant Attorney General Pottinger's conclusions regarding COINTELPRO's civil rights trespasses were announced: There was no basis for any criminal charges against those involved in the COINTELPRO operations. However, Pottinger stated that the committee had not reviewed all of the more than 60,000 pages of COINTELPRO documents; a complete review of all the documents might still lead to criminal charges against those involved, which would include present or former FBI officials.[19]

Later in January 1975 the Senate created the Select Committee on Intelligence Activities. It was authorized to investigate "the extent, if any, to which illegal, improper, or unethical activities were engaged in . . . in carrying out any intelligence or surveillance activities by or on behalf of any agency of the federal government."[20] The bureau cooperated with the committee for the many months of hearings.

Edward Levi became attorney general on February 7, 1975, replacing William Saxbe, who had resigned to become an ambassador to India. About two months later, FBI director Kelley presented Levi with some surprising news. After an exhaustive search of its investigative files, the bureau had discovered five more counterintelligence programs. Kelley brought the information to Levi, who in turn told members of various congressional committees. Investigators were now dealing with not seven but twelve COINTELPROs, although the newly discovered ones were much narrower in scope than the others. One was directed toward radical Puerto Rican independence groups, which included thirty-seven actions between August 1960 and April 1971; two concerned organized crime and the Communist party, known as "Operation Hoodwink"; and the remaining two were classified secret foreign-intelligence programs that involved twelve actions.

The actions "against Puerto Rican independence groups included the mailing of anonymous letters to the groups and furnishing information to news media, including supplying embarrassing information about an independence group leader to a television station."[21]

In Operation Hoodwink, there had been four anonymous mailings— including a letter to an alleged organized-crime figure along with an article attacking labor practices at the individual's place of business, which was made to appear as if it had been written by Communist Party U.S.A. officials.

The Senate and House Select Committees on Intelligence Activities, headed by Senator Frank Church and Representative Otis Pike, conducted the most extensive study and analysis of the U.S. intelligence establishment ever conducted. Some information on COINTELPRO became public during the hearings. The *New York Times*, in an editorial dated June 28, 1975, said that "the FBI's counterintelligence programs seemed to have been almost too crude to believe."[22]

By July 23, 1975, Church Committee investigators had access to the "full unexpurgated file on COINTELPRO." In another *New York Times* article, writer John M. Crewdson discussed the expanding COINTELPRO revelations and noted that Attorney General Levi called some of the FBI actions "outrageous" and "foolish." Crewdson went on to say that "the prospect of indicating the FBI agents in connection with COINTELPRO or break-ins is bound to place some strain on the relationship between the bureau and the [Justice] Department."[23]

The *New York Times* reported that the FBI had conducted about 1,500 break-ins in the name of domestic intelligence. The break-ins included embassies, missions, and "headquarters of extremist groups such as the Ku Klux Klan and the American Communist Party."[24]

The work of the original Senate Select Committee on Intelligence Activities finished its investigation on April 28, 1976. The report was extensive.[25] It discovered "a pattern of reckless disregard of activities that threatened our constitutional system." Indeed, the Church Committee Report pulled no punches in its narrative. All the COINTELPRO methodologies were graphically explained in case-by-case method. The report, which required extensive cooperation from all of the intelligence agencies under review, put extra strain on the FBI.

In testifying on January 26, 1976, before a different congressional committee—the Senate Committee on Government Operations—FBI Director Clarence Kelley testified that for months the FBI had undergone a most exhaustive review of its intelligence operations and that the bureau had been in regular contact with Attorney General Levi regarding counterintelligence activities. Kelley emphasized that access to sensitive information must remain limited.

Kelley asked the senators if they thought the country would benefit from continuing to permit direct congressional access to FBI information. Or would it be better served by requiring all FBI directors to be accountable to an oversight committee through sworn testimony? The director's opinion was that the Congress and the FBI would best fulfill their separate responsibilities by the latter means.

Kelley pointed out that, in responding to requests of the two select committees, FBI headquarters' staff alone had expended 3,976 days of agent personnel and 1,964 days of clerical personnel from April through December 1975. This represented manpower diverted from FBI investigative duties. The cost was about $640,500. Additionally, the cost of conducting background investigations of committee staff members had reached $393,699. Many requests from Congress were duplicates. Though the FBI tried to respond accurately in each instance, it was an expensive, time-consuming operation. Kelley felt that the interests of the American people would be best served if Congress consolidated its oversight functions into one joint committee.[26]

In 1977, as part of the information disclosure and reorganization of domestic intelligence operations, the Congress established permanent intelligence oversight committees in the House of Representatives and the Senate.

On April 5, 1976, Attorney General Edward Levi's guidelines for domestic security and intelligence investigations became the bureau's standard operating procedure. The Levi guidelines were intended to prevent a recurrence of COINTELPRO-type operations. According to the comptroller general's assessment of November 9, 1977, "they remedied many problem areas because they clearly distinguished between the different phases of an investigation—preliminary, limited, and full field—in terms of the duration and scope of investigation, and the investigative techniques permitted." In addition, the attorney general created the Investigations Review Unit "to monitor and review the FBI's domestic intelligence and counterintelligence operations." Under the Levi guidelines, the FBI could initiate a domestic intelligence investigation "of groups or individuals whose activities are directed toward the overthrow or serious impairment of Government operations or the obstruction of citizen's civil rights with slightly less substantive information than is required to initiate a criminal investigation." However, Levi specified that "government monitoring of individuals or groups because they hold unpopular or controversial political views is intolerable in our society." The guidelines allowed domestic intelligence investigations and the lawful use of informants for the purpose of facilitating criminal investigations and to anticipate violence, but clearly stated that "no one is subject to full domestic security investigation unless he or she is directly involved in violence or engaging in activities which indicate he or she is likely to use force or violence in violation of a federal law."[27]

On April 1, 1976, Attorney General Levi announced that creation of a special review committee within the Department of Justice to contact persons who may have been victimized by improper and questionably legal COINTELPRO actions. They would be notified that they had been subjects of COINTELPRO activities. Notification would be limited to those who the Justice Department thought had in some way been wrongfully harmed by COINTELPRO action.

The notifications were to be mailed by the newly formed Office of Professional Responsibility, which was part of the Justice Department. These letters, which were generally delivered by U.S. marshals, were brief and to the point: "A review of FBI files ordered by the attorney general indicates that you may have been affected by an FBI counterintelligence program in [date]. If you would like to receive more information concerning this matter please send a written request specifying the address to which you want this material mailed."[28]

Michael E. Shaheen, Jr., head of the Office of Professional Responsibility, advised the Congress and the news media that individual COINTELPRO victims would "receive all the information contained in the FBI's file, including field office proposals for actions against them, the headquarters approval, other FBI communications involving the cases and the record on whether the actions were successful or failed. The names of informants will be deleted."[29]

The COINTELPRO victim notification program represented, according to the Church Committee, "an important step toward redressing the wrongs done."

In a further effort to put the consternation over COINTELPRO to rest, FBI Director Kelley apologized to the American public "for abuses of the bureau's investigative powers in the 'twilight' of J. Edgar Hoover's career." In an effort to bring the controversy to a close, he addressed the COINTELPRO issue directly in a speech at Westminister College in Fulton, Missouri, on May 8, 1976.

> During most of my tenure as director of the FBI, I have been compelled to devote much of my time attempting to reconstruct and then to explain activities that occurred years ago.
>
> Some of those activities were clearly wrong and quite indefensible. We most certainly must never allow them to be repeated. It is true that many of the activities being condemned were, considering the times in which they occurred, the violent sixties, good-faith efforts to prevent bloodshed and wanton destruction of property.[30]

On August 11, 1976, Clarence Kelley transferred domestic intelligence investigations to the General Investigative Division, where they would be managed like all other criminal cases in that division. The transfer affected investigations of the Communist Party U.S.A., the Socialist Workers party, and all other domestic-security investigations. Under the new guidelines governing FBI activities, all such investigations would be reviewed periodically by the attorney general.[31] On November 21, 1977, under the authority of the Freedom of Information Act, the FBI released some 52,000 pages related to the twelve COINTELPROs—the entire file known at that time.

The Kelley reforms reflected the director's basic "quality over quantity" investigative philosophy. The scope of FBI intelligence investigations before the Kelley reforms was so broad-based that the General Accounting Office found them to be ultimately unproductive. Kelley's main concern was using the bureau's intelligence resources to meet two basic needs: to prevent terrorist crimes, and to "assist future investigations of specific criminal acts." The COINTELPRO operations and the resulting bad publicity undoubtedly provided much of the motivation and direction for the Kelley intelligence reorganization. FBI domestic security operations were, to use political scholar John T. Elliff's phrase, brought "down to manageable dimensions." Indeed, to again quote Elliff, "the domestic security guidelines brought an end to forty years of FBI investigations of lawful political activities, conducted in the name of protecting the government from remote, speculative threats of revolutionary overthrow."[32]

Thus, the FBI intelligence establishment had undergone significant reform by 1976. The various congressional investigations had exposed the COINTELPRO operations in considerable detail, and these exposures led to the establishment of the Levi guidelines and the Kelley reorganization.

The overall results were dramatic. In a study completed on June 30, 1977, the comptroller general reported that, in just two years' time, the FBI pending domestic-intelligence investigative matters decreased from 9,814 to 642. The number of domestic-intelligence cases initiated decreased from 1,454 to 95.

In 1974 the FBI investigated 157 organizations in the name of domestic intelligence; by mid–1977 the number was down to seventeen organizations and groups. In March 1975 the FBI had 788 special agents involved in domestic intelligence and related investigations; by midsummer of 1977 the total was down to 143. In November 1975 the bureau was utilizing about 1,100 undercover informants in domestic intelligence; by midyear 1977 it was using only about 100.[33]

A 1982 study by the U.S. Senate Committee on the Judiciary revealed that, as a direct result of the domestic intelligence reforms, only thirty-eight current domestic security investigations were in progress, which included twenty-two organizations and sixteen individuals.[34]

FBI Director William Webster, who became director in 1978, testified before a congressional committee and said that the Levi guidelines had a substantial effect in reducing FBI domestic case loads. He also said, "Investigations on 'rank and file' members [of targeted organizations] were discontinued, some where shifted to the Foreign Counterintelligence Guidelines, and others were closed with new emphasis on quality over quantity." Webster went on to say that he preferred to "retain the character of domestic security investigations as essentially criminal investigations—as established by the criminal standards of the Levi guidelines—rather than as intelligence investigations."

Although the COINTELPRO operations officially ceased to exist in 1971, the news media have maintained a strong interest in the controversial programs until the present day.

In the November 22, 1977, *New York Times*, Jo Thomas reported on the more than 500 newly released COINTELPRO documents that outlined the ten-year campaign against Puerto Rican separatist parties.[35] This COINTELPRO, which targeted party members in New York and Puerto Rico, was created to disrupt "parties which seek independence for Puerto Rico through other than lawful means." In one of the originating memos, J. Edgar Hoover sent the following instructions to special agents involved in this COINTELPRO:

> The Bureau believes this program can be effective [wrote Hoover to the special agent-in-charge (SAC), San Juan] and we suggest that the following tactics be employed . . . the use of informants to disrupt the movement and create dissension within the groups . . . the use of handwritten letters to plant the seeds of suspicion between various factions . . . the use of anonymous mailings concerning Puerto Rico's relationship with the United States to be sent to subjects within the independence movement who may be psychologically affected by such information.

Undercover informants were instructed "to report even the slightest bits of information concerning the personal lives of Puerto Rican separatists." In one situation Juan Mari Bras, one of the leaders of the Puerto Rican Socialists, had been the subject of an FBI disruption effort. The target suffered a serious heart attack, which special agents saw as a "positive result" of their efforts.[36]

A dentist in New York, known to be sympathetic to Puerto Rican independence, was the subject of an anonymous letter sent to New York State officials by the bureau. The deliberately ungrammatical letter said that the dentist was practicing without a license and asked, "Why don you stop this man from hurt the Spanish people?"[37]

In total the bureau monitored the political activities of more than 150 Puerto Rican separatist leaders including those who headed the Puerto Rican Independence Movement, the Puerto Rican Socialist party, the University Students for Independence, and High School Students for Independence.

By using acrimonious anonymous telephone calls and letters, the bureau sought to create tension between independence groups. One former employee of the San Juan FBI office—Gloria Teresa Caldas de Blanco—

has revealed that special agents were intercepting and reading the mail then being addressed to independence militants and leaders. According to a *New York Times* interview with a former FBI official, these COIN-TELPRO-type operations continued until at least mid–1974.

In March 1981 the U.S. Justice Department agreed to pay $10,000 to each of five persons whose constitutional rights had been violated by the FBI. The illegal bureau actions included "wiretaps, burglaries, or mail openings in the early 1970s."

One individual, Sara Blackburn, had her telephone tapped and her residence broken into, chiefly because she had once contributed to the Black Panthers. Another target, Lewis Cole, was a leader of the SDS disorders at Columbia University in 1968 and 1969.[38]

Also in 1981, Isaiah J. Poole wrote an article for the September issue of *Black Enterprise* entitled "Harking Back to COINTELPRO." Poole expressed black wariness concerning COINTELPRO fully ten years after its end. "Some blacks perceived," Poole wrote, "shades of COINTEL-PRO when Attorney General William French Smith told a breakfast meeting of reporters that there was an 'early warning system' that would alert the administration to outbreaks of racial disorders that would occur as a fallout of cuts in special programs."[39]

In March 1983 the Federal Bureau of Investigation began a counter-intelligence investigation that seemed to some ominously similar to COINTELPRO. This new program again threatened the First Amendment rights of U.S. citizens.

On March 30, 1983, an intelligence memorandum from FBI headquarters in Washington instructed eleven FBI field offices to investigate "the involvement of individuals and the CISPES [Committee in Solidarity with the People of El Salvador] organization in international terrorism as it affects the El Salvadorian government and [authorized] the collection of foreign intelligence and counterintelligence information as it relates to the international terrorism aspects of this investigation."[40]

Eventually, the CISPES investigation involved fifty-two of the bureau's fifty-nine field offices. The bureau focused its attention on more than 160 political organizations that were perceived by FBI officials as supporting international terrorism in Central America—that is, "organizations sympathetic to leftist guerrillas in El Salvador."[41]

The bureau's investigation was closed after a Justice Department review in 1985, and it came to national attention when 1,200 pages of FBI intelligence documents were provided to the Center for Constitutional Rights through the Freedom of Information Act in 1988. These documents demonstrated quite clearly that special agents utilized undercover informants, photographed individuals participating in peaceful demonstrations, photographed the license plates of those attending demonstrations, and also maintained surveillance on activist college students known to support CISPES.

Organizations mentioned in the documents included the Southern Christian Leadership Conference, the Maryknoll Sisters, the United Automobile Workers, the Knights of Columbus, the New Institute of Central America, the Arizona Refugee Project, the University Baptist Church in Seattle, Michigan Interfaith, the Committee on Central American Human Rights, and the East Bay Sanctuary in Berkeley.

"Now, as in earlier incidents," Gary M. Stern wrote in 1988, "purely political activity became the subject of an extensive investigation by the FBI."[42]

According to one confidential memo concerning CISPES, special agents "deemed it imperative . . . to formulate some plan of attack against CISPES and specifically against individuals . . . who defiantly display their contempt for the U.S. Government."[43]

Raymond K. DeHainaut, advisor to the Tampa CISPES, recalls that he was visited on several occasions by FBI special agents between 1980 and 1985. They visited DeHainaut at his University of South Florida campus ministry chapel and told him several times that "CISPES national leaders were unsavory characters with long histories as left wing activists and trouble makers." On other occasions he was told that CISPES was really an idea of Fidel Castro. DeHainaut, who knew that he was certainly within his constitutional rights to oppose Reagan administration policies in Central America, said that the FBI visits "were systematic and followed a familiar pattern of subtle and not-so-subtle harassment."[44]

Joseph Lowry, president of the Southern Christian Leadership Conference, became incensed that "in the 80's we have the FBI wasting taxpayers' money to harass, intimidate, or discredit organizations that have long histories of the highest patriotism."[45]

Sister Mary Ellen Merten, spokeswoman for the Maryknoll Sisters, was "quite surprised that the FBI would want to investigate a group such as ours who work with local church leaders in 28 countries around the world."[46]

During the period 1980–85 the office of the New Institute of Central America, located in the Old Cambridge Baptist Church in Cambridge, Massachusetts, was burglarized four times; the Arizona Refugee Project in Phoenix was burglarized twice. The University Baptist Church in Seattle was broken into, as was the office of Michael Lent, national program coordinator for CISPES. Many other offices—all headquarters for groups associated with CISPES—were also burglarized. The pattern was chillingly consistent. "[I]mportant papers are stolen or rifled while money and valuables are left untouched."[47]

In 1986, David Lerner of the Center for Constitutional Rights said, "It's reminiscent of the COINTELPRO era. These incidents suggest some form of official sanctioning or even government involvement."[48]

The FBI denied this strongly, emphasizing that it was motivated by the search for criminal activity, not the investigation of political beliefs.

Nevertheless, in September 1988 FBI Director William S. Sessions "imposed disciplinary sanctions against six FBI employees involved in a controversial investigation of a political group that opposed United States policies in Central America."[49]

After a lengthy investigation into the CISPES matter, the Senate Select Committee on Intelligence concluded that "the CISPES case was a serious failure in FBI management, resulting in the investigation of domestic political activities that should not have come under governmental scrutiny. It raised issues that go to the heart of this country's commitment to the protection of constitutional rights. Unjustified investigations of political expression and dissent can have a debilitating effect upon our political system. When people see that this can happen, they become wary of associating with groups that disagree with the government and more wary of what they say or write."[50]

The most significant judicial decision on the FBI's COINTELPRO practices came on August 25, 1985. U.S. District Court Judge Thomas Griesa released a 210-page decision upholding the right of the Socialist Workers party and the Young Socialist Alliance to publicize their political views and to participate in political activity "free from interference and monitoring by the FBI or other agencies of the government."[51]

The Socialist Workers party received $42,500 "for disruption activities by the FBI, $96,500 for surreptitious entries by the FBI, and $125,000 for the FBI's use of informants."[52]

It would seem that the COINTELPRO story should have ended in 1976.

As we have seen, it has not necessarily ended.

The reforms of FBI policy regarding domestic counterintelligence activities were completed by 1976. After 1976, virtually any FBI counterintelligence investigation affecting constitutional rights should have been known by the director of the FBI and by various assistant directors, section chiefs, branch chiefs, supervisors, and special agents. The attorney general, members of the Senate FBI Oversight Committee, and—perhaps to a lesser degree—the president would be apprised.

The machinery set up to monitor the FBI's domestic counterintelligence activities did not function properly in the CISPES case. An extensive investigation of citizens engaged in entirely lawful political activity lasted for at least two years.

Richard E. Morgan, an expert in constitutional law, addresses the matter of ongoing COINTELPRO-like operations: "Domestic intelligence activity is a legitimate law enforcement activity, and, as such, it must be conducted within the parameters of Constitutional law. Activities like the FBI's COINTELPRO operations and harassment of dissenters should end, and warrant requirements for electronic or physical searches should be observed."[53]

The United States, as the oldest republic in the world, should know as much or more than any nation on earth about protecting individual liberties. America's more-than-two-centuries-old Constitution would certainly seem to attest to this. However, the matter of protecting the Constitution remains exceedingly difficult—utilizing the machinery of government to protect liberties without losing them in the process.

The COINTELPRO operations were initially designed with all the good intentions in the world. However, the programs were soon being run without accountability to anyone outside of the bureau. Interestingly enough, the only act that stopped the COINTELPROs was, of all things, an illegal act: the Media office burglary.

Supreme Court Justice Louis Brandeis sounded a warning that is perhaps more meaningful today than when it was written in 1928: "The greatest dangers to liberty lurk in insidious encroachment by men of zeal, well-meaning but without understanding."[54]

NOTES

1. Unpublished letter, Carl Stern (law correspondent, NBC News) to author, 15 Jan. 1991.

2. Letter, Carl Stern to Deputy Attorney General Richard Kleindiest, 20 Mar. 1972.

3. Letter, Carl Stern to Deputy Attorney General Ralph E. Erickson, 26 June 1972; Letter, Deputy Attorney General to Carl Stern, 21 Aug. 1972.

4. Letter, Carl Stern to Acting Director of the FBI L. Patrick Gray, 6 Sept. 1972.

5. FBI Memorandum, Director Clarence M. Kelley to All Special Agents-in-charge, Personal Attention Memorandum 56–73, 5 Dec. 1973.

6. Federal Bureau of Investigation, Press Release, 7 Dec. 1973.

7. Letter, Carl Stern to FBI Director Clarence M. Kelley, 7 Dec. 1973.

8. Letter, FBI Director Clarence M. Kelley to Carl Stern, 26 Dec. 1973.

9. Unpublished letter, Sen. Sam J. Ervin, Jr., to FBI Director Clarence M. Kelley, 8 Feb. 1974.

10. Clarence M. Kelley and James Kirkpatrick Davis, *Kelley: The Story of an FBI Director* (Kansas City, Mo.: Andrews, McMeel, and Parker, 1987), pp. 179–80.

11. Department of Justice Memorandum, Henry E. Petersen to the Director of the Federal Bureau of Investigation, 24 May 1974.

12. Kelley and Davis, *Story of an FBI Director*, p. 181.

13. Kelley and Davis, *Story of an FBI Director*, pp. 181–84; FBI Memorandum, J. J. McDermott to Mr. Jenkins, 12 Nov. 1974; FBI Memorandum, Director to the FBI Executive Committee, 7 Nov. 1974.

14. House Committee on the Judiciary, Civil Rights and Constitutional Rights Subcommittee, *Hearings on FBI Counterintelligence Programs*, 93rd Cong., 2d sess., 20 Nov. 1974, p. 12.

15. Department of Justice, Press Release, 18 Nov. 1974.

16. Statement of FBI Director Clarence M. Kelley, 18 Nov. 1974.

17. Kelley and Davis, *Story of an FBI Director*, p. 186; "Kelley Vows to Restrict Counterintelligence Acts," *New York Times*, 4 Dec. 1974, p. 52.

18. Warren Weaver, Jr., "Limits on Power of FBI Proposed," *New York Times*, 1 Dec. 1974, p. 30.

19. "Charges over FBI's Tactics on Subversive Suspects Barred," *New York Times*, 4 Jan. 1975, p. 7.

20. Senate Select Committee to Study Governmental Operations with Respect to Intelligence Activities, 94th Cong., 2d sess., 14 Apr. 1976.

21. Department of Justice, News Release, For Immediate Release, 25 May 1975.

22. "Disruption by Stealth," *New York Times*, 28 June 1975, p. 34.

23. John M. Crewdson, "The Attorney General Is Going from One Crisis to Another," *New York Times*, 20 July 1975, p. 3.

24. "FBI Embassy Break-ins Put at One-a-month Rate," *New York Times*, 21 July 1975, p. 27.

25. Richard Gid Powers, *Secrecy and Power, The Life of J. Edgar Hoover* (New York: Macmillan, 1986), p. 487.

26. Kelley and Davis, *Story of an FBI Director*, pp. 87–88.

27. Report of the Comptroller General of the United States, *FBI Domestic Operations: An Uncertain Future*, 9 Nov. 1977, pp. 11–14; John T. Elliff, *The Reform of FBI Intelligence Operations* (Princeton, N.J.: Princeton University Press, 1979), pp. 55–64.

28. Jerry Oppenheimer, "Notification Process to Begin for Targets of FBI's COINTELPRO," *Washington Star*, 12 May 1976, p. 83.

29. Ibid.

30. "Apology Is Given by Head of FBI," *New York Times*, 9 May 1976, p. 26.

31. Kelley and Davis, *Story of an FBI Director*, p. 189.

32. Elliff, *Reform of Intelligence Operations*, p. 190.

33. U.S. General Accounting Office, *Comprehensive Statement on the Federal Bureau of Investigation's Conduct of Domestic Intelligence Operations under the Attorney General's Guidelines*, 9 Nov. 1977, pp. 16–19.

34. Senate Select Committee on the Judiciary, Subcommittee on Security and Terrorism, *Impact of Attorney General's Guidelines for Domestic Security Investigation*, 98th Cong., 1st sess., Nov. 1983, p. 5.

35. Jo Thomas, "Documents Show FBI Harassed Puerto Rican Separatist Parties," *New York Times*, 22 Nov. 1977, p. 26.

36. William Lichtenstein and David Wimhurst, "Red Alert in Puerto Rico," *Nation*, 3 June 1979, pp. 780–81.

37. Jo Thomas, "Harassed Puerto Rican Separatist Parties," p. 26.

38. Peter Kihss, "5 Gain Settlements for FBI Acts in the '70's," *New York Times*, 16 Mar. 1981, p. 1.

39. Isaiah J. Poole, "Harking Back to COINTELPRO," *Black Enterprise* (Sept. 1981): 25.

40. Gary M. Stern, *The FBI's Misguided Probe of CISPES*, Center for National Security Studies, CNSS Report No. III, Washington, D.C., June 1988, p. 1.

41. "Bad Habits Die Hard," *Time*, 8 Feb. 1988, p. 33.

42. Stern, *Misguided Probe*, p. 2.

43. Charles Colson, "Who's Afraid of Hanoi Jane?" *Christianity Today*, 8 April 1988, p. 64.

44. Raymond K. DeHainaut, "The FBI's Political Intimidation," *Christian Century*, 27 Apr. 1988, p. 420.

45. "FBI Spies," *Christian Century*, 24 Feb. 1988, p. 184.

46. Ibid.

47. Alfie Kohn, "The Return of COINTELPRO?" *Nation*, 25 Jan. 1986, p. 74.

48. Ibid., p. 75.

49. Barbara Bradley, "FBI Chief Disciplines Agents for Misconduct," *Christian Science Monitor*, 15 Sept. 1988, p. 3.

50. Senate Select Committee on Intelligence, *The FBI and CISPES*, 101st Cong., 1st sess., July 1989, Committee Print, p. 1.

51. "A Fight for Political Rights," Political Rights Defense Fund, New York, 1986, p. 54.

52. Ibid.

53. Richard E. Morgan, *Domestic Intelligence: Monitoring Dissent in America* (Austin: University of Texas Press, 1980), p. 124.

54. Quoted in Anthony Lewis, "The Men of Zeal," *New York Times*, 24 May 1973, p. 45.

Bibliography

Blackstock, Nelson. *COINTELPRO: The FBI's Secret War on Political Freedom*. New York: Pathfinder, 1988.

Cowan, Paul, Nick Egleson, and Nat Hentoff. *State Secrets: Police Surveillance in America*. New York: Holt, Rinehart & Winston, 1974.

Dellinger, Dave. *More Power than We Know*. Garden City, N.Y.: Anchor Press, 1975.

Demaris, Ovid. *The Director: An Oral Biography of J. Edgar Hoover*. New York: Harper's Magazine Press, 1975.

Divale, William Tulio, with James Joseph. *I Lived inside the Campus Revolution*. New York: Coles Book, 1972.

Donner, Frank J. *The Age of Surveillance*. New York: Alfred A. Knopf, 1980.

Drury, Allen, and Fred Maroon. *Courage and Hesitation*. Garden City, N.Y.: Doubleday, 1971.

Ehrlichman, John. *Witness to Power*. New York: Simon and Schuster, 1982.

Elliff, John T. *The Reform of FBI Intelligence Operations*. Princeton, N.J.: Princeton University Press, 1979.

Fain, Tyrus G., Katharine C. Plant, and Ross Millay. *The Intelligence Community*. New York: R. R. Bowker, 1977.

Felt, Mark. *The FBI Pyramid*. New York: G. P. Putnam's Sons, 1979.

Halperin, Morton H., Jerry J. Erman, Robert L. Borosage, and Christine M. Marwick. *The Lawless State: The Crimes of U.S. Intelligence Agencies*. New York: Penguin Books, 1976.

Hampton, Henry, Steve Fayer, and Sarah Flynn. *Voices of Freedom: An Oral History of the Civil Rights Movement from the 1950's through the 1980's*. New York: Bantam Books, 1990.

Jayko, Margaret, ed. *FBI on Trial*. New York: Pathfinder, 1988.

Johnson, Lyndon B. *The Vantage Point: Prospectives of the Presidency, 1963–1969*. New York: Holt, Rinehart & Winston, 1971.

Kelley, Clarence M., and James Kirkpatrick Davis. *Kelley: The Story of an FBI Director*. Kansas City, Mo.: Andrews, McMeel, and Parker, 1987.

Morgan, Richard E. *Domestic Intelligence: Monitoring Dissent in America*. Austin: University of Texas Press, 1980.

Morison, Samuel Eliot. *The Oxford History of the American People*. New York: Oxford University Press, 1965.

Navasky, Victor S. *Kennedy Justice*. New York: Atheneum, 1977.

O'Reilly, Kenneth. *Racial Matters: The FBI's Secret War on Black America, 1966–1972*. New York: Free Press, 1989.

Perkus, Cathy, and Noam Chomsky. *COINTELPRO: The FBI's Secret War on Political Freedom*. New York: Monad Press, 1975.

Powers, Richard Gid. *Secrecy and Power, The Life of J. Edgar Hoover*. New York: Macmillan, 1986.

Schlesinger, Arthur M., Jr. *The Crisis of the Old Order*. Boston: Houghton Mifflin, 1957.

———. *The Imperial Presidency*. Boston: Houghton Mifflin, 1973.

Shannon, David A. *The Decline of American Communism*. Chatham, N.J.: Chatham Bookseller, 1959.

Sidey, Hugh. *A Very Personal Presidency: Lyndon Johnson in the White House*. New York: Atheneum, 1968.

Sullivan, William C., with Bill Brown. *The Bureau: My Thirty Years in Hoover's FBI*. New York: W. W. Norton, 1979.

Theohoris, Athan. *Spying on Americans: Political Surveillance from Hoover to the Huston Plan*. Philadelphia: Temple University Press, 1978.

Unger, Sanford J. *FBI: An Uncensored Look behind the Walls*. Boston: Little, Brown, 1975.

Welch, Neil J., and David W. Marston. *Inside Hoover's FBI*. Garden City, N.Y.: Doubleday, 1984.

White, Theodore H. *Breach of Faith: The Fall of Richard Nixon*. New York: Atheneum, 1975.

———. *The Making of the President 1964*. New York: New American Library, 1966.

———. *The Making of the President 1968*. New York: Atheneum Publishers, 1969.

————. *The Making of the President 1972*. New York: Atheneum Publishers, 1973.

Whitehead, Don. *Attack on Terror: The FBI against the Ku Klux Klan in Mississippi*. New York: Funk & Wagnalls, 1970.

Wise, David. *The American Police State*. New York: Random House, 1976.

Index

ABOUT THE AUTHOR

JAMES KIRKPATRICK DAVIS is President of Davis Advertising Agency Inc. in Kansas City, Missouri. A student of American history for 30 years, Mr. Davis worked directly with Clarence Kelly, former Director of the FBI, as co-author of the book *Kelley: The Story of an FBI Director*.